Sew-Easy
Designer Pillows™

Edited by Barbara Weiland

HOUSE of
WHITE
BIRCHES
PUBLISHERS
SINCE 1947

Sew-Easy Designer Pillows

EDITOR	Barbara Weiland
ART DIRECTOR	Brad Snow
PUBLISHING SERVICES MANAGER	Brenda Gallmeyer
ASSOCIATE EDITOR	Dianne Schmidt
ASSISTANT ART DIRECTOR	Nick Pierce
COPY SUPERVISOR	Michelle Beck
COPY EDITORS	Nicki Lehman, Mary O'Donnell, Beverly Richardson
TECHNICAL ARTISTS	Allison Rothe, Leigh Maley
GRAPHIC ARTS SUPERVISOR	Ronda Bechinski
BOOK DESIGN	Amy S. Lin
GRAPHIC ARTISTS	Glenda Chamberlain, Edith Teegarden
PRODUCTION ASSISTANTS	Cherly Kempf, Marj Morgan, Judy Neuenschwander
PHOTOGRAPHY	Tammy Christian, Don Clark, Matthew Owen, Jackie Schaffel
PHOTO STYLISTS	Tammy Nussbaum, Tammy M. Smith
PUBLISHING DIRECTOR	David J. McKee
MARKETING DIRECTOR	Dan Fink
EDITORIAL DIRECTOR	Gary Richardson

Printed in China
First Printing: 2006
Library of Congress Control Number: 2005930128
Hardcover ISBN-10: 1-59217-097-8
Hardcover ISBN-13: 978-1-59217-097-5
Softcover ISBN-10: 1-59217-131-1
Softcover ISBN-13: 978-1-59217-131-6

1 2 3 4 5 6 7 8 9

Pick a Pillow!

Pillows, pillows everywhere and so many beautiful ones from which to choose! That's what I see when I thumb through the pages of this exciting new book. If your rooms need refreshing or updating with color and design, you are sure to find the perfect pillow shape and design amidst the projects in this book. From simple squares to neck rolls and cushions in unusual shapes, there's a size and style that will add interest to a chair, sofa or bed—or even the floor.

I think of pillows as the perfect sewing project because:

- Most pillows require easy-to-cut geometric shapes.
- Pillows don't require much fabric, so you can splurge a bit on the materials and still save a bundle.
- Pillows are usually less than 24 inches square, so they require minimal cutting and sewing time.
- Pillow construction is easy, with most designs requiring basic straight-line stitching skills. They're great for beginners.
- Pillows don't require any fitting adjustments.
- Pillows give you the opportunity to play with color and trims without a major investment in time or materials.
- Pillows are the perfect canvas for showcasing a special fabric or textile treasure.
- Pillows can reflect your own personal style and color sense.

All in all, pillows are little gems that add the finishing flourish to decorating schemes in any room of the house. The return on your investment in time and materials is well worth the time it takes to stitch a beautiful pillow. While you might be able to purchase pillows in similar shapes, styles and fabrications, most decorator pillows would carry price tags of $50 and up in retail shops, decorator showrooms or from online or mail-order sources.

I hope you enjoy making new designer pillows for every room in your house using the directions that follow. We've included a section with basic pillow construction techniques along with some tips from the pros to guarantee success. So, sit back with a cup of your favorite beverage while you flip through the following pages to find a design that appeals to you. Then have fun shopping for the perfect fabrics and trims to complement your decor. Of course, you are free to substitute fabric types and colors for the ones shown to suit your decorating scheme and personal taste. With fabrics and trims at hand and the step-by-step directions close to your machine, have fun making designer pillows that you will be proud to display in your home for years to come.

Barbara

Barbara Weiland

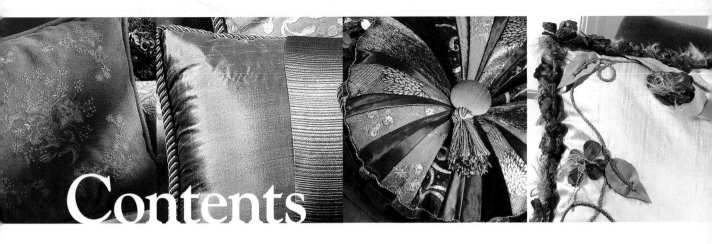

Contents

Let's Make a Pillow

Pillow Components

To create a pillow, you will need two essential ingredients—fabric and a pillow form of the appropriate size and shape. You may also need a zipper, hook-and-loop tape, snap tape or buttons for the back closure. In addition, many pillows require an edge finish. Purchase twisted-cord welting, fringe or other trim for the outer edge, or make your own welting with cotton cable cord and fabric.

• First determine the size and shape of the pillow you want to create, and then buy the appropriate pillow form or create your own following the directions on this page.

• Purchase and prepare the desired fabric and the required trims and notions, and your pillow will soon be finished. You can also adapt the basic directions below in addition to the directions for individual projects in this book to create pillows of your own design.

• You will need some basic sewing tools and equipment. Before

you get started, be sure to read through Necessary Tools & Notions on page 21.

Pillow Forms

Pillow forms are widely available in numerous standard sizes and shapes at fabric stores. Choose a knife-edge form, a three-dimensional foam cushion or a bolster/neck roll depending on your pillow design. Most knife-edge pillow forms consist of an outer cover filled with loose polyester fiberfill; some are feather-filled.

Note: *If the form you choose is too plump or firm for the look* *you wish to create, you can undo the stitching and remove some of the filler before restitching the layers together.*

In some home dec departments, you can have foam forms cut to the specific size required. If you must custom-cut a foam cushion yourself, use an electric knife for best results. For extra-thick cushions, it may be necessary to glue two layers of foam together to create the desired size.

Another option for custom sizes and shapes is NU-Foam, a relatively new product from Fairfield processing. This dense polyester-fiber product can be easily cut to size with scissors or a bread knife (see Ships Ahoy Step 11 on page 93, for cutting how-tos).

You can also create your own knife-edge pillow insert using muslin or a similar cotton fabric for the cover and polyester fiber-fill for the stuffing. This step is essential when you are making pillows that vary from the available standard sizes and shapes.

Making a Knife-Edge Form

1. Determine the desired finished size and shape of the pillow form, and draw it on a double layer of muslin. Add ½-inch-wide seam allowances to all edges. Cut out two identical pieces for the form cover.

2. Sew the pieces together, leaving an opening in one edge for stuffing.

3. Turn right side out and stuff to the desired firmness. Machine-stitch the opening edges together (Figure 1 on page 8). If the form is too firmly stuffed to machine-stitch,

whipstitch the edges together by hand, using strong thread for added security.

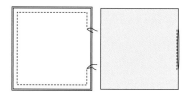

Figure 1
Sew muslin layers together.
Turn right side out and stitch
opening edges together.

Making a Box-Edge Form

1. Follow the directions for the knife-edge form to mark and cut the front and back panels from muslin or similar weight woven fabric.

2. For the boxing-strip width for the side panel, measure the cushion depth and add 1 inch

Use It Again

You can recycle the filling in worn pillows or use an existing knife-edge pillow to stuff a new one.

• If the pillow cover has no zipper or back opening and it's the correct size for the pillow you are making, simply use the existing pillow as the pillow form.

• If the pillow cover is worn and has no opening, cut the cover open and remove the stuffing. If it has become matted, use your fingers to fluff and renew the fibers before using them to fill a new pillow form that you create following the directions for making pillow inserts.

for seam allowances. For the length of the boxing strip, add the length and width of the pillow-top panel and multiply by two. Add 1 inch for the seam allowances. Use these dimensions to cut a muslin strip. If necessary, cut more than one strip and piece together to make a strip of the correct length.

3. Join the ends of the long boxing strip and press the seam allowance open.

4. Beginning with the seam at the center on one long edge, pin and stitch one raw edge of the boxing strip to one of the pillow panels. Clip the boxing strip at the corners for smoothly turned corners (Figure 2).

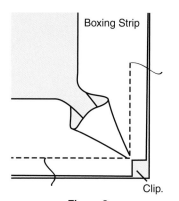

Figure 2
Clip boxing-strip seam allowance
to turn smooth corners.

5. Repeat with the remaining panel, *leaving an opening in one long edge for turning and stuffing.* After stuffing, machine-stitch the opening edges together as shown in Figure 1 for a knife-edge cushion.

Fabric Selection & Preparation Components

Check out the pillow section in any home furnishings department and you'll find pillows made from almost every fabric imaginable—silk dupioni, cotton corduroy, velvet, organza, taffeta, faille, synthetic suede, cotton prints and wovens—to name a few. Beautiful ribbons and trims can be transformed into pillow tops too. Cotton quiltmaking fabrics are available in a wonderful array of solids, tone-on-tone prints and thousands of other printed designs. These fabrics are not as sturdy as decorator cottons from the home dec department, but they offer you countless additional choices. Almost anything goes for pillow decor, as long as it is suitable for the look you want to achieve.

The designers for this book chose a variety of fabrics for their designs. Several of the pillows were made using silk dupioni, which is often available in both the fashion fabric and home dec fabric departments. It's a favored fabric for its interesting texture and brilliant colors. Of course you can substitute other fabrics for a different look.

Don't overlook fabrics that might not be typically considered pillow fabric. Fashion fabrics intended for apparel are also options to consider. Some of them will definitely require stabilizing (see Stabilizing Fabrics on this page).

Adding a fusible interfacing to the wrong side of lightweight or delicate fabrics will add the required stability and durability. This type of backing may be an essential component for loosely woven fabrics that ravel. It is recommended for silk dupioni in particular, and many of the projects in the following pages include it.

Fabric Preparation

1. If you plan to launder your finished pillow cover, it is essential to wash and dry the fabrics before you begin. If you are using stain-resistant fabrics from the home dec fabric department, dry cleaning is recommended instead of laundering to preserve the finish. However, decorator cottons do wash and dry beautifully if laundering the pillow cover is desirable.

2. Straighten the cut ends by pulling a thread or cutting along a visible thread. For nonwoven fabrics such as synthetic suede and knits, use rotary-cutting tools to straighten the cut edges so they are perpendicular to the selvages.

3. If necessary, apply fusible interfacing to the wrong side of the cut pieces before proceeding with the construction as directed.

Stabilizing Fabrics

If the fabric you've chosen needs added stability or durability, back the pieces with a lightweight fusible interfacing.

1. Choose a light- to medium-weight knit, woven or weft-insertion fusible interfacing. These types have the most flexibility after fusing and will create a more natural look. Test your interfacing options on fabric scraps first.

2. Read the manufacturer's directions and follow the recommended procedure. Usually you will need a press cloth, an iron and moisture to ensure a permanent bond. In addition, it may be essential to press and fuse again from the fabric right side.

3. Allow the pieces to cool before you begin sewing.

Note: If you plan to machine-embroider a motif on a pillow top as shown on the pillow on page 74, apply fusible interfacing to the wrong side of the fabric piece before sewing. This may eliminate the need for additional embroidery stabilizer. Be sure to do a test stitchout on interfacing-backed scraps to make sure it is adequate. If not, place a layer of cut-away or tear-away stabilizer under the fabric, and then hoop both layers in preparation for embroidering.

Pillow Construction Techniques

If you've never made a pillow, it's essential to review the following directions before you begin your pillow project. Refer back to them as needed while you make your pillows. If you're an experienced sewer, use the tips and techniques to improve your sewing, make pillow sewing easier and create projects with a professional decorator look. Be sure to check out the Tricks of the Trade on page 19 for some insider tips for professional results.

Seam Allowances

In home dec projects, the standard seam allowance is ½ inch wide. However, in this book pillows that feature patchwork-style construction may have ¼-inch-wide seam allowances instead. If the fabrics ravel, it's a good idea to stitch the seams, and then zigzag- or serge-finish the seam allowances together after each step.

Cutting & Joining Fabric Strips

Bias-cut strips may be required for binding, piping or welting, or other sections of a pillow top. Because bias stretches, it's important to handle it carefully. To cut true-bias strips, rotary-cutting equipment is essential.

A long ruler with a 45-degree-angle line makes it easy to start the cuts; the measuring lines allow you to cut accurate widths across the fabric after the first diagonal cut is made.

Cutting Bias Strips

1. Begin with a piece of fabric that has been straightened along the grainline on two adjacent edges. Use a single layer, or fold larger pieces in half with straight-grain or selvage edges aligned.

2. Position the fabric on the cutting mat and smooth out any wrinkles. Place the 45-degree-angle line along the straight or folded edge at the widest part of the fabric and make the first cut (Figure 3).

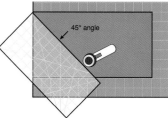

Figure 3
Make the first bias cut.

3. Use the appropriate line on the ruler to align and cut the fabric into strips of the required length (Figure 4).

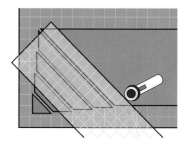

Figure 4
Cut strips of the required width.

Note: *Mark the desired width on the underside of the ruler with neon tape or narrow masking tape to make it faster and easier to find and position the ruler for the desired width.*

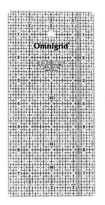

Sewing Bias Seams

If the strips for welting, piping or binding were cut on the bias, the angled ends are on the straight of grain. To join the strips into one continuous length:

1. Make sure that the adjoining ends are cut at the correct angle (Figure 5).

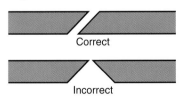

Correct

Incorrect

Figure 5
Check cut ends for the correct angle.

2. If the strip ends are not correctly cut, place both of them face up, one on top of the other, and re-cut one to match the other (Figure 6).

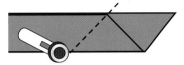

Figure 6
Stack one strip on top of the other, with right side up on both strips.

3. Place the strips right sides together with the raw edges even and small "ears" extending at each end. Stitch as shown and press the seam open (Figure 7).

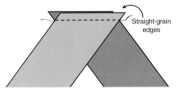

Straight-grain edges

Figure 7
Sew cut ends together.

Sewing Bias Seams in Straight-Grain Strips

When strips are cut on grain instead of the bias, the ends are square. To create a bias seam:

1. Place one strip on the other at right angles and pin.

2. Draw a diagonal stitching line and then stitch on the line (Figure 8).

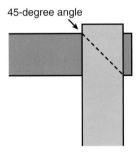

45-degree angle

Figure 8
Arrange strips and stitch the angled seam.

3. Trim the excess, leaving a ¼-inch-wide seam (Figure 9). Press the seam open.

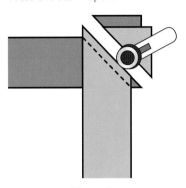

Figure 9
Trim excess, leaving ¼"-wide seam allowance. Press open.

Welting Edge Finishes

Many pillows require piping or welting as the edge finish. It may also be used to accent interior seams in some pillow designs. In the directions that follow, the term "welting" is used, but the two terms—piping and welting—are interchangeable.

To make your own matching or contrasting welting, you will need cotton cable cord for the filler. It is available in a wide range of sizes. You can decide how "fat" you want the finished edge trim or follow the designer's recommendation as listed in the materials list for the pillow you are making. Although specialty feet for making piping/welting are available for most sewing machines, a zipper foot will suffice.

Making Fabric-Covered Welting

1. Cut bias or straight-grain fabric strips at least 1 inch wider than the cable cord diameter. If you don't know the diameter, wrap a piece of paper around the cord and pin in place. Trim the excess paper ½ inch from the pin and remove the paper. Measure it for the minimum cutting width required (Figure 10).

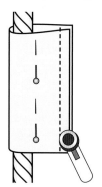

Figure 10
Wrap paper around cable cord.
Pin and trim ¹/₂" from cord.
Remove and measure paper
to determine strip width.

2. Sew the strips together to make one long strip equal to the distance around the pillow top, plus 5 or 6 inches. Use bias seams (see Sewing Bias Seams above) and press open.

3. Attach the zipper foot and adjust the foot to the right of the needle.

4. Wrap the fabric strip around the cord, right side out, and align the raw edges. Machine-baste close to the cord, keeping the cord smooth inside the fabric as you stitch (Figure 11).

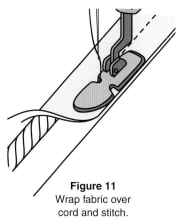

Figure 11
Wrap fabric over
cord and stitch.

Note: *To control difficult fabrics while making welting, see Marta's Welting below.*

5. If necessary, trim the seam allowance to an even ½ inch along the length of the wrapped cord.

Applying Welting

Sew the piping or welting to the completed pillow top and finish the ends as directed below.

1. Put a contrasting-color thread in the bobbin and adjust the machine for a basting-length stitch.

2. Beginning at the center of one edge of the pillow top, begin stitching the piping in place. Leave the first 2 inches unstitched to allow for joining the ends neatly. When you reach a corner, clip the piping/welting seam allowance to the stitches to turn a smooth corner. If you prefer a rounded corner, ease the piping around the corner instead (Figure 12).

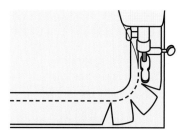

Figure 12
Clip welting seam
allowance at corners.

Marta's Welting

Some fabrics are difficult to control as you wrap them around cord to create your own welting. Marta's method solves the problem. It's particularly helpful when making welting with thick fabrics, napped fabrics or synthetic suede. Simply apply a light coat of temporary spray adhesive to the wrong side of the fabric strip before wrapping it around the cord. Finger-press the layers together, and then stitch as directed for Making Fabric-Covered Welting.

3. When you near the beginning end of the piping/welting, cut the excess, leaving at least 1 inch to overlap the first end.

4. Remove the stitching in the seam at one end and cut the cord so that it meets the other cord end (Figure 13).

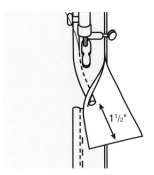

Figure 13
Cut cord to butt the first end.

5. Trim the excess fabric, leaving a ¼-inch turn-under allowance. Turn under and wrap around the cord ends. Complete the stitching (Figure 14).

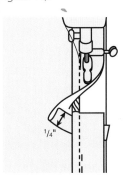

Figure 14
Turn fabric under.

Note: *For bulky fabrics, see Alternate Joining Methods.*

6. When sewing the pillow front to the completed pillow back or a boxing strip, pin the layers together with right sides facing and raw edges even. With the pillow top facing you so you can see the contrasting basting stitches, sew the layers together using the zipper foot. As you stitch, crowd the cord by stitching just inside the basting.

Note: *You may want to adjust the needle position to the left one notch so it stitches closer to the cord—if that is possible on your sewing machine. On bulky fabrics, clip the seam-allowance corners for a smoothly turned corner.*

Alternate Joining Methods

To evenly distribute the fabric thickness when applying welting covered with heavier fabrics, a bias join is preferred.

1. Follow steps 1 and 2 as directed in Applying Welting.

2. When you reach the beginning of the welting, cut away the excess, leaving a 2-inch overlap.

3. Undo the stitching and trim the cord inside the overlap to meet the beginning cord end.

4. Trim the fabric end on the true bias, leaving a ¼-inch-wide turn-under allowance.

5. Turn under the allowance and wrap the end over the welting end with cord ends butting. Complete the stitching (Figure 1).

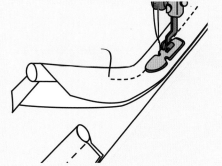

Cut cord to butt. Cut fabric at 45-degree angle and turn under ¼".
Wrap around both cords.

Another way to join ends is to cut both ends so they butt together, and then wrap them with matching fabric (or ribbon or flat trim) as directed in the Road to Marrakech pillow on page 60 before completing the stitching.

Applying Twisted-Cord Piping
Some pillows require ready-made twisted-cord piping instead of fabric-covered welting. If you prefer, you can substitute this decorator trim for custom-made welting to create a different look. Joining the ends can be done in several ways. Whenever you cut a length of twisted cord, first wrap the area with a piece of masking tape and cut through the center (Figure 15).

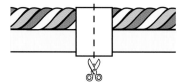

Figure 15
Wrap twisted cord with
tape before cutting.

1. Position the corded piping with the piping seam allowance in the pillow-top seam allowance. Attach the zipper foot and adjust the machine for a basting-length stitch.

2. Begin at the center at the bottom edge of the pillow top and start the stitching 2 inches from the beginning. Stitch as close to the cord as possible.

3. Choose one of the following methods to join the corded piping ends neatly.
• The easiest join is the butted and fabric-covered option shown on page 60 in the Road to Marrakech pillow.
• Another option, which works best for the smaller cord trims, is to overlap the ends on an angle when you reach the point where they meet (Figure 16). Trim the excess cord and seam allowance even with the pillow-top edge.

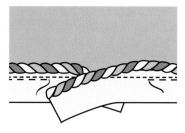

Figure 16
Overlap ends of corded
piping. Stitch and trim ends
even with seam edge.

• For larger trims, the least noticeable join is achieved by untwisting and realigning the cords in the trim.

a. Sew the cording to the pillow top as directed for welting on page 12. Allow for at least a 2-inch overlap where the piping meets (Figure 17a).

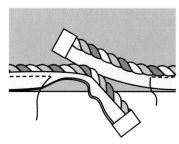

Figure 17a

b. Snip the stitches that hold the cord to the seam-allowance tape to free about 1½ inches of the cord at each end. Overlap the ends of the seam-allowance tape by 1 inch and trim away any excess seam allowance (Figure 17b).

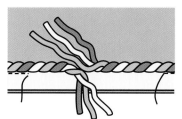

Figure 17b

c. Turn the right-hand cord ends down on one end of the loosened piping and secure with a piece of cellophane tape (Figure 17c).

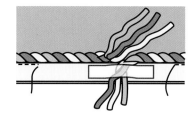

Figure 17c
Turn cord ends down and
tape to seam allowance.

d. Turn the left-hand cord ends down and arrange the cord ends to continue the cord.

Check to make sure that the rearranged and overlapped cords looks the same on the underside, and then tape the cords in place (Figure 17d).

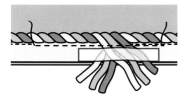

Figure 17d
Align remaining cords
for a continuous join.

e. Complete the piping stitching and trim the excess cord even with the seam-allowance raw edge.

Note: *The cords in some twisted-cord piping lie in the opposite direction of that shown in Figures 17a, b, c and d. In that case, simply reverse steps c and e.*

Closures

Each pillow in this book features a closure appropriate for the design as chosen by the designer. In general, there are three basic pillow closures: zippers, lapped-back envelope closures, or a stitched opening. The first two allow for easy removal of the cover for cleaning or when you want to quick-change the pillow cover for a new look without discarding the pillow form. Back closures can usually be interchanged as you prefer.

The stitched closure requires hand stitching the opening edges together. The disadvantage of this closure is that you must undo the stitches to remove pillow cover for cleaning, and then restitch it after replacing the pillow form. However, this closure may be the best option in some pillow designs due to shape or construction.

For zipped closures, use a lapped zipper unless you prefer the smooth look of an invisible zipper. The centered zipper application is often used in boxing strips for cushions.

For truly reversible pillows, use an invisible zipper (page 16) in one of the seams, or leave an opening for inserting the pillow and then hand-sew the opening closed (page 19).

Lapped Zipper Application
Lapped zippers are a standard closure in decorator pillows. The lapped closure results in a tailored finish and hides the zipper teeth and pull on the wrong side of a pillow that is not meant to be reversible. You may place the lapped zipper closure wherever you wish. In most pillows with a directional design orientation on the front, the zipper is placed at the upper or lower edge of a pillow. In either case, the edge of the overlap should face downward (Figure 18).

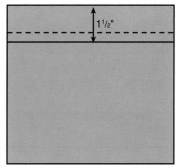

Top Placement

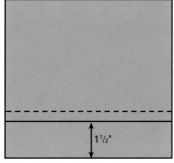

Bottom Placement

Figure 18
Lapped zipper placement
in pillow back.

When zippers are required for the pillows in this book, ¾-inch-wide seams are included in the cutting dimensions for the back pieces. If you are creating your own pillow size, this is the recommended allowance for best results. It allows for a wider placket than you would stitch in a garment, and this makes it easier to stitch past the bulk of the zipper pull to avoid a "bump" in the stitching.

Note: *The directions that follow illustrate a back panel with a lapped zipper placed close to what will be the bottom edge of the pillow. For closure with the zipper toward the upper edge, the fabric panels (wide and narrow)* *would be in reverse positions in the illustration. The method shown varies slightly from what is normally shown for a lapped zipper in a dress so that the zipper will unzip from left to right on the back of the pillow and the lapped edge will face downward.*

1. Sew the two panels together, changing to a basting-length stitch for the zipper opening. Backstitch at the ends of the seam before changing to the basting stitch. After returning to the standard stitch length, stitch forward a few stitches, then back to lockstitch the seam (Figure 19).

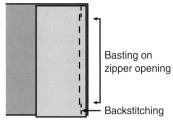

Basting on
zipper opening

Backstitching

Figure 19
Sew back panels together
to prepare for zipper.

2. Press the seam open. Fold the pillow lower panel toward the right side of the larger panel so only a seam allowance extends to the right (Figure 20).

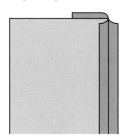

Figure 20
Stitch close to zipper teeth
from top to bottom.

3. Attach the zipper foot and move it to the right of the needle. Unzip the zipper and place it face down on the lower seam allowance only. Position it with the teeth along the seam line and the upper and lower stops at the beginning and end of the basting. Stitch from the top of the zipper to the end, stitching close to the zipper coil (Figure 21).

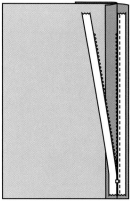

Figure 21
Stitch close to zipper teeth
from top to bottom.

4. Zip the zipper and turn it face up to expose the seam and the right side of the zipper. Move the zipper foot to the left of the needle and stitch close to the fold through all layers (Figure 22 at the top of the next column). This creates the underlap.

5. Adjust the foot position as needed. Machine-baste the remaining half of the zipper to the pillow back through all layers, stitching along the woven guideline in the zipper tape. You may continue the basting to the outer edges of the panel or you

may stitch across both ends just past the zipper stops.

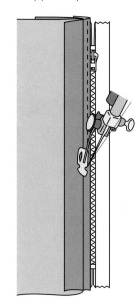

Figure 22
Edgestitch seam allowance
close to zipper teeth.

6. On the right side, machine-stitch the zipper in place, using the basting as a guide (Figure 23).

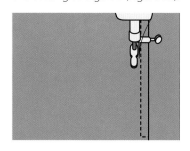

Figure 23
With foot adjusted to left of
needle stitch alongside basting.

7. Remove the basting, unzip the zipper and insert the pillow form.

Note: *For an alternate lapped zipper method that requires basting tape instead of basting stitches, see Marta's Method on page 12.*

Invisible Zipper Installation

The invisible zipper is installed *before* you sew the opening seam allowances together. For best results, use a zipper foot designed specifically for this type of zipper. Generic feet as well as brand-specific ones are available for most sewing machines. Check with your dealer.

1. Unzip the zipper and use the tip of the iron to open and flatten the natural "curl" in both halves of the zipper (Figure 24).

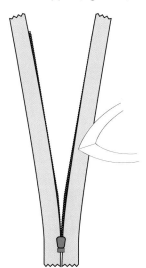

Figure 24
Unroll and press coil
to prepare for application.

2. Machine-baste ⅝ inch from both opening edges as a positioning guide.

3. Before you begin, stabilize the seam allowances on lightweight fabric to prevent puckering. Center and fuse a ½-inch-wide strip of lightweight fusible interfacing over the seam line.

4. Apply double-sided basting tape to both halves on the right side of the zipper tapes. Position the zipper face down on the right side of one piece of fabric with the edge of the coil just past the basting. Use one pin at the top to hold the zipper in place until you begin stitching.

5. Attach the invisible zipper foot to the machine and adjust so that the needle is centered in the opening. Stitch from the upper zipper stop, stopping to position the coil as you go (Figure 25). End the stitching when the zipper foot touches the slide; backstitch.

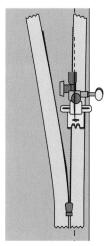

Figure 25
Position with coil edge
just past basting.

6. Place the remaining pillow-back panel face down on top of the zipper with raw edges aligned. Flip the upper corner back and pin the remaining half of the zipper to the seam allowance. Make sure the coil is just past the basting line. Position

the coil under the appropriate tunnel in the bottom of the zipper foot and stitch from the top to the bottom. Zip the zipper.

7. To complete the seams above and below the zipper, adjust the invisible zipper foot to the left of the needle or attach your regular zipper foot and adjust to the left. Fold the piece in half with seam-allowance raw edges aligned and stitch, beginning a thread or two to the left of the end of the zipper stitching. If you try to match the stitching lines, you will cause a pucker. Do not pull on the zipper tapes. Backstitch and stitch to the end of the seam (Figure 26). Repeat to complete the seam at the opposite end.

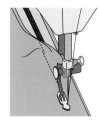

Figure 26
Start a few stitches above last
stitch and slightly to the right.

8. To prevent the zipper from stressing the stitches, sew the zipper-tape ends to the seam allowances (Figure 27).

Figure 27
Stitch both zipper tape ends
to seam allowances only.

Zipped Box Cushion Covers

If you are making a box-edge cushion, a zipper in the center of one side of the cushion edges will make it easy to insert the cushion and remove it when you want to clean the cover. Use an invisible zipper or a lapped or slot zipper application (Figure 28).

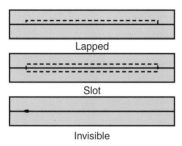

Figure 28
Zipper choices for boxing strip.

1. Cut the boxing strip the length of three adjacent sides, adding 1 inch for the seam allowances. For the zippered panel, cut the strip 1 inch longer than the pillow side and 1½ inches wider than the long strip. For example, for a 16-inch-square pillow that is 3 inches thick, you would cut one 4 x 49-inch strip and one 5½ x 17-inch strip.

2. Fold the shorter, wider strip in half lengthwise and press. Cut along the crease.

3. Insert the longest zipper possible in the strip using the desired zipper application.

4. Sew the zipper panel to the remaining long panel at both short ends. Leave the first and last ½ inch of each seam unstitched, backstitching to secure the stitching. Press the seam allowances open (Figure 29).

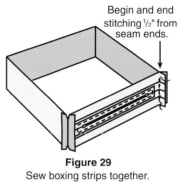

Begin and end stitching ½" from seam ends.

Figure 29
Sew boxing strips together.

5. Pin and sew the boxing strip to the pillow top and then to the pillow bottom, allowing the seams to spread at the corners (Figure 30).

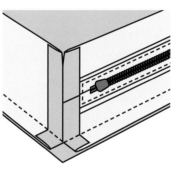

Figure 30
Sew boxing strip to pillow top.

Envelope Backs

If you really don't want a zipper in your pillow and the pillow is not meant to be reversible, choose an envelope back instead. With this method, you will need additional fabric for the second back panel required. The top layer of the envelope closure must overlap the under-layer by several inches so that the pillow form is completely encased when tucked inside. The directions for cutting and creating an envelope closure are included with each project. If the pillow you've chosen does not include an envelope closure and you would like one, follow the steps below to cut and prepare the pieces for your pillow.

1. Divide the finished size of the pillow back in half and add 3 inches for hems and overlap to each center edge. This is the new cut size for the pillow-back panels (Figure 31).

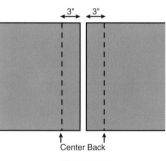

3"   3"

Center Back

Figure 31
Cut two pieces for envelope back.

2. Cut two pieces of fabric using the dimensions determined in step 1.

3. Turn under and press a 1-inch-wide hem at each overlap edge. Turn under and press again to make a double-layer hem. Stitch close to the inner edge on each overlap.

4. Overlap the layers and adjust to make a pillow back that matches the cut dimensions of the pillow front. Machine-baste the overlapped edges together ⅜ inch from the raw edges (Figure 32).

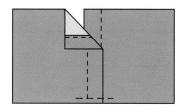

Figure 32
Overlap finished edges.

For a buttoned back closure, make buttonholes in the top layer and sew buttons in place on the underlayer before overlapping and basting. If you want a hook-and-loop closure, position and edgestitch the tapes in place in the hemmed areas before overlapping and basting the pieces together. In lieu of one long piece, you can use several small squares or dot closures.

Another closure option for envelope backs is snap tape. Edgestitch a length of it along the opening edges; then overlap and snap before machine-basting the overlapped layers together ⅜ inch from the raw edges.

Stitched Pillow Closure

1. If a zipper or envelope back is undesirable, stitch the pillow fronts and backs together leaving an opening in one edge for turning and inserting the pillow form. The larger the pillow, the larger the opening. Be sure to backstitch at the beginning and end of the seam to avoid stressing the stitching when inserting the form.

2. Turn the cover right side out and press under the seam allowance on one opening edge only.

3. Insert the pillow form.

4. Lap the pressed seam edge over the unpressed edge and slipstitch the fold to the pillow cover. Use small stitches and doubled, waxed thread (see Tricks of the Trade) for the most secure and invisible closure (Figure 33).

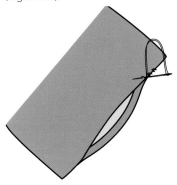

Figure 33
Slipstitch folded edge to remaining seam allowance along seam line.

Tricks of the Trade

These tips will help you improve the appearance of your pillows for truly professional results.

For Better Covered Buttons

Whenever possible, choose covered-button forms that are made of plastic rather than shiny metal. If you must use a metal form, prevent the metal from showing through by applying a layer of lightweight fusible knit or woven interfacing to the wrong side of the fabric circle first.

For More Perfectly Turned Square Corners

When you turn square or rectangular pillow covers right side out and push out the corners, they can become distorted. For really square corners, try this trick. It may look like it won't work, but give it a try. You'll be surprised at how it can improve the appearance of square corners.

1. On the wrong side of the pillow top, draw intersecting seam lines at each corner.

2. Pin the pillow front to the pillow back and stitch together; when you are within a few inches of the marked seam line, begin tapering inside the line (Figure 34). Pivot at the corner and reverse the tapering.

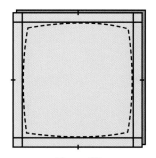

Figure 34
Use marked ½" seam lines as guides to stitch slightly bowed corners.

Another strategy is to stop stitching within an inch of the marked corner and adjust the stitch length to 18 stitches per inch. Continue stitching, stopping just shy of the corner so you can do a half pivot and take two short stitches across the point. Make another half pivot, stitch for 1 inch, and then return to the normal stitch length until you are within 1 inch of the next corner (Figure 35). Repeat the process at each corner. The few stitches across the corner make more room for the seam allowance to fit smoothly inside the turned pillow cover. The shorter stitches add durability to the corners.

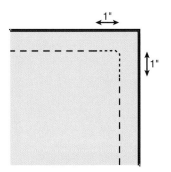

Figure 35
Shorten stitches and
stitch across corner.

For a Snug Fit

Loose pillow covers are unattractive and detract from a truly finished look—unless you are going for a softer, more cushiony pillow. Try these methods to achieve a snug fit and smooth pillow.

• For a snug fit, cut the pillow cover pieces the desired finished size—instead of adding seam allowances all around. In this book, this technique has been used by several of the designers to ensure a good fit. Don't panic if you see that the cut size for a 16-inch pillow top is 16 or 16½ inches instead of 17 inches, which would allow for ½-inch-wide seam allowances all around. When you insert the pillow form of the desired finished size into a slightly smaller cover, it will be a snug fit, ensuring that the cover is smooth and taut across the pillow form inside.

• An alternate method is to cut the cover pieces including the ½-inch-wide seam allowances, and cut matching pieces of thin cotton batting. Use temporary spray adhesive to adhere the batting to the wrong side of each piece or machine-baste it in place. The added batting layers help fill out the pillow cover to perfection.

• If your completed pillow cover still fits loosely and you want a snug look, remove the pillow form and wrap it in a layer of batting. Use spray adhesive to adhere the layers to the form or use catchstitches to sew the butted edges of the batting together. Reinsert the form. This method is often an essential step to fill out box-edge pillow covers.

For Stronger Hand-Sewing Thread

When hand sewing, use two layers of thread run through a cake of beeswax. After coating the threads, lay them between two layers of paper towel and press with a hot iron. This melts the wax into the thread so it won't rub off as you draw it through the fabric over and over as you stitch.

To Fix Wimpy Corners

Often when you insert a knife-edge pillow form into the completed cover, the corners are never as plump and filled as the rest of the cover. It's usually impossible to force the corners of the form into the pillow-cover corners to fill them out as desired. However, there's an easy fix. Fill out flat or wimpy corners by tucking bits of polyester fiberfill into them after you have inserted the pillow form.

Necessary Tools & Notions

The three most essential tools for pillow making include a sewing machine, a serger (optional but nice for seam finishing and controlling fabric edges that ravel) and an iron. In addition, sharp shears and measuring tools are necessary. For professional pillow-making results, you should have the following tools and supplies on hand in your sewing room:

Batting: Adding a layer of lightweight cotton or cotton-blend quilt batting is a great strategy for adding bulk to a pillow covering, whether it has quilted details or not. The extra layer will help fill out the cover for a firm, smooth fit. See Tricks of the Trade on page 19.

Buttonhole Twist: Use for attaching buttons to tufted cushions and pillows.

Fusible Interfacing: Use fusible interfacing to "beef up" lightweight fabrics for better wear and to control raveling on fabrics such as silk dupioni (see Stabilizing Fabrics on page 9). It is also an excellent stabilizer for pillow pieces that will be embellished with machine embroidery.

Fusible Web: Use to apply trims and embellishments to the pillow surface. It can also act as a substitute for machine- or hand-stitching openings closed.

Hook-&-Loop Tape: Use as a closure on envelope closures (page 18) in pillow backs. Apply a strip the length of the finished opening edges, or apply small squares in two or more evenly spaced locations along the back closure edges. You may substitute snap tape if you wish.

Marking Tools: You will need a pencil, air- or water-erasable marking pen, and/or dressmaker's chalk for marking cutting and stitching details. Which one to use will depend on the task and the fabric you are using. See the individual pillow projects for specific instructions from the designers.

Pattern tracing paper or cloth: Use this gridded paper or cloth when drafting pattern pieces.

Pins: Quiltmaking pins are longer—usually 1¼ inches—and are ideal for controlling the multiple layers encountered in home dec projects. Opt for fine, glass-head dressmaking pins when working with delicate fabrics. When quilting layers together, substitute small safety pins for straight pins to hold the layers together—or use temporary spray adhesive (see page 22).

Polyester Fiberfill: Use to stuff muslin covers for custom-made knife-edge or box-edge pillow forms.

Pressing Equipment: Keep a seam roll or seam board with a point presser handy at the ironing board for pressing seams in otherwise difficult-to-reach areas. A press cloth is essential for fusing interfacing to pillow fabrics, as well as when using fusible web. It is also essential for protecting some fabrics surfaces, such as suede and velvet, as well as synthetic fabrics and metallic accents from damage from the iron heat.

Rotary-Cutting Tools: Use these tools in place of shears and pattern pieces to cut perfectly accurate geometric shapes and bias or straight-grain strips for welting and other trim details.

Sharp Shears & Scissors: Use whenever rotary-cutting

equipment is not available or not appropriately sized for the cutting task. Opt for rotary cutting whenever possible for smooth, clean cuts and accurate dimensions.

Tapes: Use masking tape or cellophane tape to secure trim ends and prevent unraveling when cutting them (see page 14). Use double-sided basting tape to secure zippers and trims for stitching.

Temporary Spray Adhesive: Use to adhere fabric and batting layers together when quilting a pillow top as discussed in Tricks of the Trade. Or, use it to adhere fabric to welting when making your own welting for pillow edges and trim (see Marta's Welting on page 12).

Wooden Chopstick: Use to turn smooth corners in knife-edge pillow covers without poking a hole in the fabric or breaking the stitches in the seams. This can take the place of a point turner if you don't have one in your sewing tool box. It also comes in handy for poking polyester fiberfill into pillow-form covers before filling the remainder of the cover.

Zipper Foot: Although other specialty presser feet may also be handy for pillow making, the adjustable zipper foot (or a piping or welting foot) is essential for inserting zippers and for making and attaching welting and ready-made twisted-cord piping. ◆

Trimly
Tailored

Squares and rectangles are the most traditional pillow shapes and the easiest to sew. Even a simple shape covered in a beautiful fabric with a bit of piped edging can add drama and texture to any setting, but open yourself to the other trim and finishing ideas shown on the pillows in this section to create personalized versions of these trim and tailored styles.

Gold Rush

DESIGNS BY PAM ARCHER

For dazzling pillows with a look of luxury, opt for these little gems. Pair the rich sheen of silk with accent fabrics to create a trio of elegant and opulent looks for far less than the price of one small nugget.

Finished Sizes

Gold Standard: 14 x 16 inches
Gold Filigree: 18 inches square
Golden Feathers: 12 x 16 inches

Gold Standard

Materials for Gold Standard

- 44/45-inch-wide fabric
    - ⅝ yard gold silk dupioni for pillow front and back
    - ⅞ yard gold stripe, rib or jacquard coordinate
- 1¾ yards ½-inch-diameter gold cord trim
- ⅝ yard lightweight batting
- 1 yard fusible knit interfacing
- 14 x16-inch pillow form
- Seam roll or point presser
- All-purpose thread to match fabrics
- Zipper foot
- Rotary cutter, mat and ruler
- Basic sewing tools and equipment

Instructions

Project Note: *Use ½-inch-wide seam allowances unless otherwise directed.*

Cutting for Gold Standard

• From the gold silk, cut one 14 x 18-inch rectangle for the pillow front. Cut two 11½ x 14-inch rectangles for the pillow back with envelope closure.
• From the gold coordinate fabric, cut one 13 x 28-inch strip for the decorative band.
• From the fusible knit interfacing, cut one 14 x 18-inch rectangle for the pillow front and two 11½ x 14-inch rectangles for the pillow back. Cut one 13 x 28-inch strip for the decorative band.
• From the lightweight batting, cut one 14 x 18-inch rectangle and two 10 x 14-inch rectangles.

Assembly for Gold Standard

1. Following the manufacturer's directions, apply the fusible interfacing to the wrong side of each corresponding piece of gold silk.

2. Pin the batting to the wrong side of the pillow front. Machine-baste a scant ½ inch from the raw edges and trim the batting close to the basting.

3. Position batting on the wrong side of each piece of silk for the pillow back with 1½ inches of silk extending past one long edge on each piece. Machine-baste a scant ½ inch from the raw edges and trim the batting close to the basting (Figure 1).

4. Turn under and press ½ inch on the fabric extension. Turn the extension over the edge of the batting and press. Edgestitch in place through all layers (Figure 2).

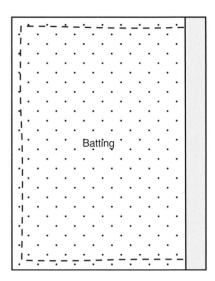

Figure 1
Machine-baste batting
to pillow back raw edges.

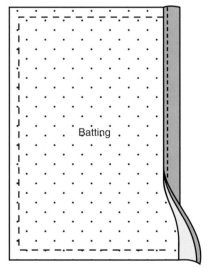

Figure 2
Wrap excess silk
over batting edge.
Stitch in place.

5. With both pillow backs face up, lap one finished edge over the other to create a 14 x 18-inch rectangle. Pin the layers together and machine baste ⅜ inch from the raw edges in the lapped area (Figure 3).

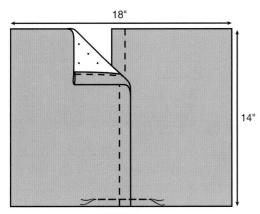

Figure 3
Stitch and baste back panels together.

6. Attach the zipper foot and adjust it to the left of the needle. Thread the bobbin with a contrasting thread. Beginning at the center of one long edge of the pillow front and leaving a 3-inch-long tail, pin and stitch the gold cord trim to the outer edges. Stitch as close to the cord as possible and make short clips in the cord lip to turn the corners smoothly as shown in Figure 12 on page 12. When you reach the starting point, curve both cords as shown in Figure 4. This join will be covered by the contrast band.

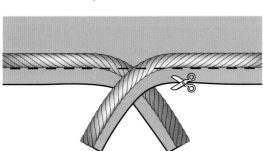

Figure 4
Curve cord ends off
the edge; trim excess.

7. With right sides together and raw edges aligned, pin the pillow back to the front. With the wrong side of the pillow front facing up, stitch through all layers, crowding the cord by stitching just inside the contrast basting as shown in Figure 11 on page 12.

8. Turn the pillow cover right side out and press only as needed. Tuck the pillow form into the pillow through the envelope opening in the back

9. Fold the strip for the contrast band in half lengthwise with right sides facing and stitch ½ inch from the long raw edges. Trim the seam to ¼ inch and press open over a seam roll or point presser.

10. Turn the resulting tube right side out, but stop when the short ends are even. Stitch ½ inch from the short end, leaving a 3-inch-long opening across the seam line for turning (Figure 5). Trim the seam allowance to ¼ inch and turn the band right side out through the opening.

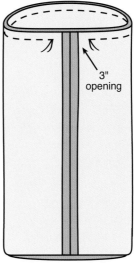

Figure 5
Fold tube into itself
with right sides together.
Stitch raw edges together.

11. Slipstitch the opening edges closed and center the seam on the back of the completed band. Press. Slip the band over the pillow and center it.

Gold Filigree

Materials for Gold Filigree

- 44/45-inch-wide fabric
    - ⅝ yard gold silk dupioni
    - ⅓ yard gold burnout drapery sheer for the filigree panels
- 2¼ yards ½-inch-diameter gold cord trim
- 18-inch-square pillow form
- ⅝ yard lightweight batting
- 1 yard 22-inch-wide fusible-knit interfacing
- Gold metallic thread
- Size 80/12 metallic needle
- All-purpose thread to match fabrics
- Optional: hook-and-loop fastener for back opening
- Zipper foot
- Rotary cutter, mat and ruler
- Basic sewing tools and equipment

Cutting for Gold Filigree

- From the gold silk, cut four 9½-inch squares for the pillow front. For the pillow back with envelope closure, cut two 14 x 18-inch rectangles.
- From the gold burnout fabric, cut two 9½-inch squares.
- From the fusible knit interfacing, cut four 9½-inch squares and two 14 x 18-inch rectangles.
- From the batting, cut one 18-inch square and two 12½ x 18-inch rectangles.

Assembly for Gold Filigree

1. Apply the fusible interfacing to the wrong side of each piece of gold silk and fuse following the manufacturer's directions.

2. Position a gold filigree sheer square face up on top of each of two of the gold silk squares and machine-baste ⅜ inch from the raw edges.

3. Arrange the gold squares in two rows and sew together. Press the seams toward the squares with the filigree overlay. Sew the two rows together to complete the pillow top. Press the seam toward the gold filigree—snipping at the center so you can change the seam allowance directions (Figure 1).

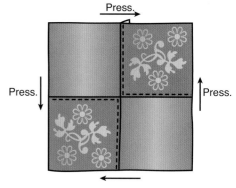

Figure 1
Sew squares together
and edgestitch.

4. Insert the metallic needle in the sewing machine and thread with gold metallic thread. Edgestitch through all layers on the gold filigree side of each seam.

5. Position the batting on the wrong side of the pillow front and machine-baste a scant ½ inch from all raw edges. Trim the batting close to the basting to reduce bulk in the seams.

6. Position batting on the wrong side of each gold rectangle with 1½ inches of fabric extending beyond one 18-inch edge of each panel. Machine-baste a scant ½ inch from the raw edges and trim the batting close to the basting. Turn under and press ½ inch on the fabric extension. Turn the fabric extension over the batting and press. Edgestitch in place through all layers (Figure 2).

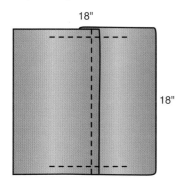

18"

18"

Figure 2
Overlap finished edges of pillow back.
Machine-baste layers together.

7. Arrange one pillow back over the other with the hemmed edges in the center, forming an 18-inch square. Pin the layers together and machine-baste ⅜ inch from the raw edges in the overlapped area as shown in Figure 2.

8. Refer to the directions for applying and joining twisted cord piping on page 14. Use contrast thread in the bobbin and the zipper foot adjusted to the left of the needle so you can stitch as close as possible to the cord. Beginning a few inches from one corner and leaving a 3-inch-long tail, sew the gold cord to the outer edge of the pillow top. Clip the cord lip as needed to turn the corners smoothly. When you reach the beginning point, create an invisible join in the cord as shown in Figures 17a, b, c, and d on pages 14 and 15.

9. With right sides facing, sew the pillow front and back together around the outer edges. Sew with the wrong side of the pillow top facing you so you can see the basting and stitch just inside it for a snug seam.

10. Turn the pillow cover right side out through the opening in the back.

11. Insert the form through the opening.

Note: *If desired, you can close the envelope back with discs of hook-and-loop tape (see page 21) or ribbon ties or frogs.*

Golden Feathers

- 44/45-inch-wide fabric
    - ¾ yard dark gold or brown silk dupioni
    - ⅜ yard gold silk dupioni
- 1⅝ yards ¼-inch-diameter dark gold cord trim
- 1⅜ yards 5-inch-long feather trim
- ⅜ yard lightweight batting
- ¾ yard 45-inch-wide fusible knit interfacing
- 12 x 16-inch pillow form
- Craft or fabric glue
- All-purpose thread to match fabrics
- Zipper foot
- Rotary cutter, mat and ruler
- Basic sewing tools and equipment

Cutting for Golden Feathers
- From the dark gold or brown silk dupioni, cut one 12 x16-inch rectangle for the pillow front. Cut two 10 x 12-inch rectangles for the pillow back with envelope closure.
- From the gold silk, cut one 8 x 25-inch strip for the decorative band with feathers.
- From the lightweight batting, cut one 12 x 16-inch rectangle for the pillow front and two 10 x 12-inch rectangles for the pillow back.
- From the fusible interfacing, cut one 12 x 16-inch rectangle and two 8½ x 12-inch rectangles for the pillow front and back. For the contrast band, cut one 8 x 25-inch strip.

Assembly for Golden Feathers
1. Following manufacturer's directions, fuse the knit interfacing pieces to the wrong side of the corresponding silk rectangles for the pillow and the silk strip for the decorative band.

2. Pin the 12 x 16-inch batting rectangle to the wrong side of the silk rectangle. Machine-baste a scant ½ inch from the raw edges. Trim the batting close to the basting. Repeat with the remaining batting pieces and the silk rectangles for pillow back, with 1½ inches of silk extending past the 12-inch edge of each piece of batting. Turn under and press ½ inch on the silk extension. Turn the extension over the raw edge of the batting and press. Stitch in place as shown in Figure 1 for the Gold Standard pillow.

3. With both pillow backs face up, lap one finished edge over the other to create a 12 x 16-inch rectangle. Pin the layers together and machine-baste ⅜ inch from the raw edges in the lapped area (Figure 1).

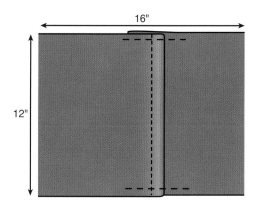

Figure 1
Lap finished edges and
baste layers together.

7. From the feather trim, cut two 24-inch-long pieces. Add a bead of craft or fabric glue on the right side of the ribbon header on one piece of ribbon. Position the ribbon under one long edge of the band and use your fingers to press it into place. Repeat with the remaining piece of trim. Allow the glue to dry completely. Topstitch ¼ inch from both long edges of the feather-trimmed band (Figure 2).

4. Attach the zipper foot and adjust it to the left of the needle. Thread the bobbin with a contrasting thread. Beginning at the center of one long edge of the pillow front and leaving a 2-inch-long tail, pin and stitch the gold cord trim to the outer edges. Stitch as close to the cord as possible and make short clips in the cord lip to turn the corners smoothly as shown in Figure 12 on page 12. When you reach the starting point, curve both cords as shown in Figure 4 for the Gold Standard pillow. The join will be covered by the contrast band.

5. With right sides together, pin the pillow front to the pillow back. With the wrong side of the pillow front facing you, stitch the layers together, stitching just inside the contrast basting. Turn the pillow cover right side out and insert the pillow through the envelope opening in the back.

6. Fold the strip in half lengthwise with wrong sides facing and stitch ½ inch from the raw edges. Trim the seam allowance to ¼ inch and press the seam open. Turn the band right side out and press, centering the seam on the underside of the band.

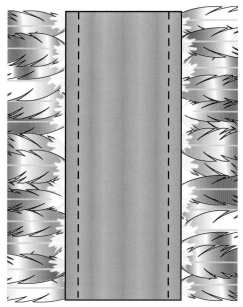

Figure 2
Topstitch ¹/₄" from
finished edges of band.

8. Serge- or zigzag-finish the short ends of the band. With right sides together, stitch the short ends together 1 inch from the raw edges. Press the seam open. Carefully turn the band right side out to protect the feathers.

9. Slide the band onto the pillow. ◆

Man-Tailored & Elegant

DESIGNS BY PAM LINDQUIST

Richly textured woolens and suedes in warm neutral tones add up to a manly pair of tailored pillows for a bedroom or den. Change the fabrics and change the mood.

Finished Sizes
Scrollwork: 18 inches square
Tailored in Suede: 18 inches square

Scrollwork

Materials for Scrollwork
- ⅝ yard 54-inch-wide houndstooth or plaid wool flannel for pillow front and back
- ¼ yard synthetic suede in coordinating color for appliqués
- 2½ yards ½-inch-wide coordinating grosgrain ribbon
- 20-inch square quilt batting
- 20-inch square muslin or other lightweight cotton fabric
- Lightweight paper-backed fusible web
- 18-inch-square knife-edge pillow form
- 16-inch-long all-purpose zipper
- All-purpose thread to match fabrics

- Press cloth
- Temporary spray adhesive
- Rotary cutter, mat and ruler
- Zipper foot
- Basic sewing tools and equipment

Cutting for Scrollwork

- From the wool flannel, cut one 19-inch square, one 8 x 19-inch rectangle and one 14 x 19-inch rectangle.
- Trace each scroll pattern on page 37 four times onto lightweight paper-backed fusible web. Leave at least ¼ inch of space between motifs. Cut out each motif with a ⅛-inch-wide margin beyond the drawn lines.
- Following manufacturer's directions, apply the fusible-web shapes to the wrong side of the suede and cut out carefully.

Assembly for Scrollwork

Project Note: *Use ½-inch-wide seam allowances unless otherwise directed.*

1. Arrange the cutouts as shown in Figure 1 on the right side of the wool-flannel square with the lowermost edges 1½ inches from the outer edges of the square. Cover with a press cloth and fuse long enough to adhere them to the wool. Stitch ⅛ inch from all raw edges of each suede appliqué.

Figure 1
Position and fuse suede
cutouts in place.

2. Apply a light coat of temporary spray adhesive to one side of the muslin square and smooth the batting in place on top. Apply another coat of adhesive to the right side of the batting. Center the appliquéd square, right side up, on top of the batting and smooth into place. Trim the excess batting and backing even with the pillow top.

3. With right sides facing, stitch the two panels for the pillow back together along one 19-inch-long edge. Use a ¾-inch-wide seam allowance and stitch the first 1½ inches. Backstitch. Change to a basting-length stitch for the center 16 inches. Backstitch. Return to the normal stitch length and complete the seam (Figure 2). Press the seam open using a press cloth on top to protect the suede.

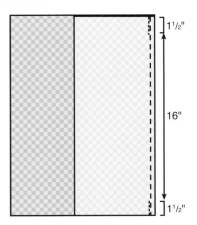

Figure 2
Stitch and baste back
panels together.

4. Insert the zipper using a lapped zipper method as shown on page 15. UNZIP THE ZIPPER.

5. With right sides facing, place the pillow top on the pillow back. Trim the back edges even with the pillow front. Sew the layers together ½ inch from the raw edges, stitching two stitches across each point rather than stitching to the point at each corner (see Figure 35 on page 20).

6. Turn the pillow cover right side out through the open zipper. Carefully press the outer edges, using a press cloth to protect the wool.

7. Beginning at one corner, position the grosgrain ribbon with one edge along the outer edge of the pillow top. Pin in place and stitch the first edge, stitching through all layers and ending at the next corner with a few backstitches. To make a mitered corner, fold in the ribbon and turn the corner referring to Figure 3. Continue framing the pillow edge in this manner until you reach the starting point. Turn under the ribbon end at a 45-degree angle to create the last miter. Trim excess ribbon.

Figure 3
Stitch ribbon to pillow outer edge;
miter ribbon at corners.

8. Stitch along the edge of each mitered fold and along the inner edge of the ribbon to make a narrow flange (Figure 4).

Figure 4
Stitch along mitered folds and
along inner edge of ribbon.

9. Insert the pillow form and tuck bits of fiberfill into the corners (see page 20) if needed to fill them out. Zip the zipper.

Tailored in Suede

Materials for Tailored in Suede

- 4 (10-inch) squares synthetic suede fabric for pillow front
- 19 x 22-inch synthetic suede rectangle for pillow back
- 16-inch-long all-purpose zipper
- Narrow strips of paper-backed fusible web
- 20-inch square thin cotton quilt batting
- 20-inch square muslin or other woven cotton
- Large decorative button, medallion, tassel or other embellishment
- 18-inch-square knife-edge pillow form
- All-purpose thread to match fabrics
- Temporary spray adhesive
- Optional: Polyester fiberfill
- Rotary cutter, mat and ruler
- Press cloth
- Zipper foot
- Basic sewing tools and equipment

Cutting for Tailored in Suede

• From the 19 x 22-inch suede rectangle, cut one 8 x 19-inch rectangle and one 14 x 19-inch rectangle.

Assembly for Tailored in Suede

Project Note: *All measurements include ½-inch-wide seam allowance unless otherwise stated.*

1. Arrange the four 10-inch suede squares for the pillow front as shown in Figure 1. Sew them together in rows. Apply fusible web to the underside of each seam allowance and finger-press open. Top the seam with the press cloth and fuse lightly—just long enough to lightly tack the seam allowances to the wrong side of the joined squares to keep them in place for topstitching.

Figure 1
Sew squares together.

2. Sew the sets of squares together to complete the pillow top; press the seams as described in step 1.

3. Apply a light coat of temporary spray adhesive to one side of the muslin square and smooth the batting in place on top. Apply another coat of adhesive to the right side of the batting. Center the suede square, right side up, on top of the batting and smooth into place. Trim the excess batting and muslin backing even with the pillow top.

4. Stitch ¼ inch from the seam lines on each side (Figure 2).

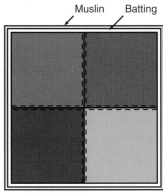

Figure 2
Topstitch ¼" from seam lines;
pivot at inner corners

5. With right sides facing, stitch the two panels for the pillow back together along one 19-inch-long edge. Use a ¾-inch-wide seam allowance and stitch the first 1½ inches. Backstitch. Change to a basting-length stitch for the center 16 inches. Backstitch. Return to the normal stitch length and complete the seam (Figure 3). Press the seam open using a press cloth on top to protect the suede.

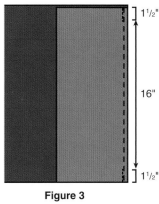

Figure 3
Stitch and baste back
panels together.

6. Insert the zipper using a lapped zipper method as shown on page 15. UNZIP THE ZIPPER.

7. With right sides facing, place the pillow top on the pillow back. Pin and stitch the front and back together ½-inch from the raw edges; stitch two stitches across each point rather than stitching to the point at each corner (see page 20). Turn the pillow cover right side out through the open zipper.

8. Carefully press the outer edges, using a press cloth to protect the suede.

9. Beginning at one corner, topstitch ½ inch from the pillow-cover outer edge, creating a narrow flange frame (Figure 4).

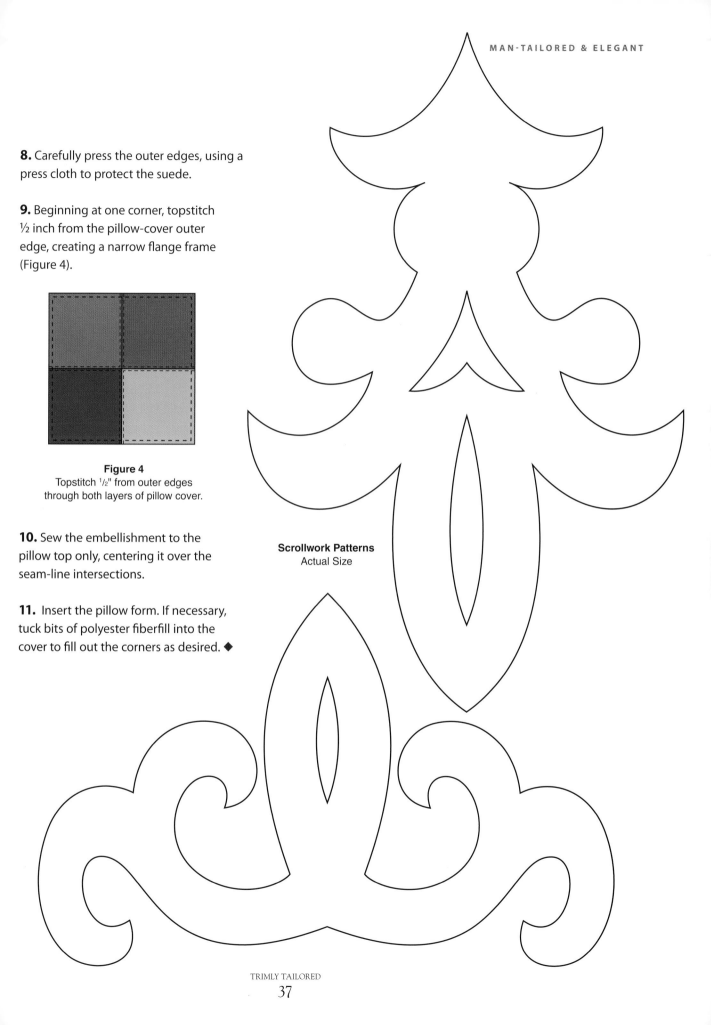

Figure 4
Topstitch ½" from outer edges through both layers of pillow cover.

10. Sew the embellishment to the pillow top only, centering it over the seam-line intersections.

11. Insert the pillow form. If necessary, tuck bits of polyester fiberfill into the cover to fill out the corners as desired. ◆

Scrollwork Patterns
Actual Size

Framed Jewels

DESIGN BY BARBARA WEILAND

Showcase a piece of antique ribbon, fabric or trim in the center of a special pillow like one of these. Silken borders and flat piping surround the center "jewel." Additional embellishments can include quilting, beads, piping or ribbon trim.

Finished Sizes

All Buttoned Up: 18 inches square
Watery Garden: 18 inches square
World in a Spin: 14½ x 17¾ inches
Note: *Your pillow size may vary depending on the fabric you choose for the centerpiece and the border widths you add.*

Materials

Note: *Yardages will vary depending on the layout you choose and the special fabric piece you choose for the center. Determine appropriate yardages as you work through the planning outlined in the step-by-step directions below.*

- 1 scrap special fabric or ribbon for the centerpiece
- Approximately ¾ yard 1 or more colors silk dupioni or similar fabric for the borders and the pillow back
- Silk scraps for the flat piping
- Optional: White, off-white or black scrap of tulle for centerpiece
- ¼-inch-wide strips of paper-backed fusible web
- Knife-edge pillow form (purchased or custom-made to fit non-standard pillow sizes as shown on page 7)
- Zipper for the back closure
- Press cloth
- All-purpose thread to match fabric
- Graph paper and pencil
- Basic sewing tools and equipment

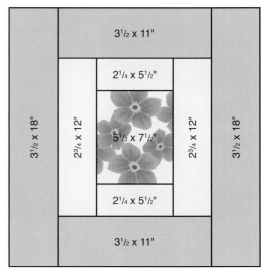

Figure 1b
Watery Garden
All dimensions are finished sizes. Add ¼" seam
allowances to all edges for cutting dimensions.
(Flat piping not shown.)

Assembly

1. Choose the fabric for the pillow center and decide how large you want it to be. Use the pillow layouts shown in Figure 1 as cutting guidelines and adjust as needed for the piece of fabric you want to showcase; your dimensions may not match exactly any of the three panels shown in the layouts. Draw out the desired arrangement of the center panel and borders on graph paper and note the *finished sizes* of each piece as shown in the illustrations.

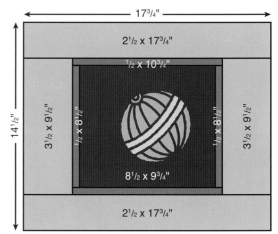

Figure 1c
World in a Spin
All dimensions are finished sizes. Add ¼" seam
allowances to all edges for cutting dimensions.

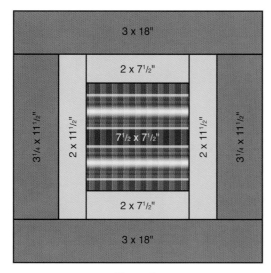

Figure 1a
All Buttoned UP
All dimensions are finished sizes. Add ¼" seam
allowances to all edges for cutting dimensions.

2. Add ¼-inch-wide seam allowances to each edge of each piece in the layout, and cut the pieces from the desired fabrics for the panel and the borders.

3. If the center fabric panel is a delicate antique, cut a matching piece of tulle in a color that fades into the background when placed over the fabric. Use black tulle on dark colors and white or off-white on lighter colors. Position the tulle over the right side of the panel and machine-baste a scant ¼ inch from all raw edges.

4. Refer to Figure 2 for steps 4 and 5. Optional: For flat piping to frame the centerpiece, cut fabric strips 1¼ inches wide and the length of the sides of the centerpiece you've chosen. Fold the strips in half lengthwise with wrong sides facing and press.

5. Pin a flat piping strip to two opposite edges of the center panel and machine-baste a scant ¼ inch from the raw edges (Figure 2).

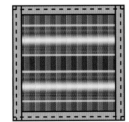

Figure 2
Sew flat piping strips
to center panel.

6. Tuck strips of ¼-inch-wide fusible web under the flat piping and fuse to the center panel. Cover the work with a press cloth to protect the fabrics from excessive iron heat. Fusing the flat piping keeps it flat and in place after you insert the pillow form into the finished pillow cover. Cut and add strips to the remaining raw edges and baste. Fuse in place with fusible web.

7. Following the layout you have chosen or created, cut two border strips for the top and bottom borders. Pin and sew to the center panel and press the seams toward the borders. Repeat to add the inner borders to the remaining opposite sides of the panel (Figure 3).

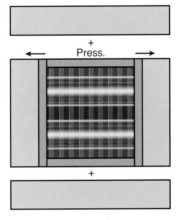

Figure 3
Add inner borders.

8. Optional piping: If your pillow design has two different borders and you want to frame the borders in trim as shown in the All Buttoned Up pillow, add purchased decorative cord piping to two opposite edges of the panel at this point.

9. Cut and add outer borders to two opposite edges of the center panel. (Use a zipper foot to stitch as close to the piping cord as possible if you are framing the piece in piping.) Press the seam allowances toward the center panel.

10. Optional piping: Apply decorative cord piping to the long edges of the panel.

11. Cut and add outer borders to the long edges of the panel. Press the seams toward the center panel.

12. If desired, add purchased cord (All Buttoned Up) or custom-made piping (Watery Garden pillow) to the outer edges of the pillow cover as shown on page 12. For a ribbon-edge flange, see World in a Spin Variations below.

13. Prepare a pillow back to match the size of the pillow front. Make an envelope closure as shown on page 18 or insert a lapped zipper following the directions on page 15.

14. If you have used a zipper in the pillow back, UNZIP THE ZIPPER. Pin the pillow cover to the pillow back with right sides facing. Stitch ¼ inch from the outer edges. Zigzag- or serge-finish the seam allowances together.

15. Turn the completed pillow cover right side out. Add buttons or other embellishments to the pillow top as desired.

16. Insert the pillow form into the cover. ◆

World-in-a-Spin Variations

This pillow features a narrow flange created by using ribbon to bind the outer edges.

1. Optional: After adding the inner and outer borders to the center panel, position and stitch narrow ribbon along the seam lines between the two borders as shown in the photo.

2. Complete the pillow top and pillow back and layer them with wrong sides together. Machine baste 3/8 inch from the raw edges.

3. Position and stitch 1-inch-wide grosgrain ribbon in place along the basting on two opposite edges. Turn the

remaining ribbon to the back over the seam allowance and pin in place. The ribbon edge should extend past the first stitching. From the right side, stitch in the ditch next to the ribbon edge, catching the ribbon in place on the underside (Figure 4).

Figure 4
Bind short edges with ribbon first.
Add top and bottom ribbons and turn short
ends under before turning ribbon to the underside.

4. Bind the remaining edges with ribbon, turning in the short ends of the ribbon at the corners for a neat finish.

Note: *This pillow also features machine quilting in the borders for added textural interest. Use the serpentine stitch on your machine and space them evenly using the edge of the presser foot as a guide.*

Color Caravan

DESIGNS BY LINDA TURNER GRIEPENTROG

Black is the perfect backdrop for the gypsy-bright colors in these exciting floor pillows. Choose your favorite jewel tones for the patches, pieces and tabs. Silk dupioni is the fabric shown, but other dressy synthetics, cottons and linens can be substituted.

Finished Sizes
Jeweled Windows: 24 inches square
Stacked & Stitched: 24 inches square
Tabs & Tassels: 24 inches square

Jeweled Windows

Materials for Jeweled Windows
- ⅞ yard 54-inch-wide black silk dupioni or similar fabric of your choice
- ¼ yard each 9 colors 45-inch-wide silk dupioni
- ¾ yard lightweight batting
- All-purpose black thread
- 24-inch-square pillow form
- Optional: ¼ yard ½-inch-wide hook-and-loop tape
- Temporary spray adhesive
- Rotary cutter, mat and ruler
- Basic sewing tools and equipment

Cutting for Jeweled Windows
- From the black silk dupioni, cut two 17 x 25-inch rectangles for the pillow back. From the remaining fabric, cut six 3 x 6-inch strips and two 3 x 20-inch strips for the sashing; also cut two 3½ x 20-inch strips and two 3½ x 25-inch strips for the borders.
- From the colored silks, cut a total of 25 assorted strips each 2 x 13 inches.

Assembly for Jeweled Windows

Project Note: *Use ½-inch-wide seam allowances unless otherwise directed.*

1. Arrange the colored silk strips in five groups of five strips each, varying colors between groupings.

2. Stitch each group of strips together and press the seam allowances in one direction in each unit.

3. Using the rotary cutter, mat and ruler, cut each strip-pieced unit into two 6-inch squares (Figure 1). There will be one extra square, as only nine are needed for the pillow front.

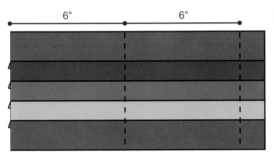

6"   6"

Figure 1
Make 5 strip-pieced units.
Cut 2 (6") squares from each one.

4. Arrange the squares in three rows of three squares each, alternating the strip directions (Figure 2).

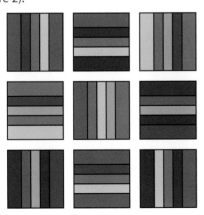

Figure 2
Arrange squares in rows.

5. Refer to Figure 3 for steps 5, 6 and 7. With right sides together, stitch the sashing and squares together in rows. Press the seams toward the sashing strips.

6. Sew the block rows together with the 3 x 20-inch sashing strips between them.

7. Pin and sew the 3 x 20-inch side borders to the panels; press the seams toward the borders. Add the 3½ x 25-inch borders to the top and bottom edges.

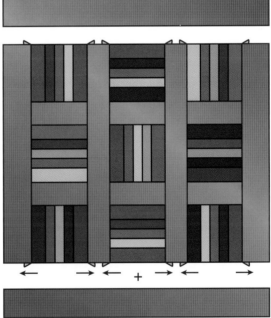

Figure 3
Arrange the squares with sashing and
sew together. Press as directed by arrows.

8. To prepare the lapped pillow backing, turn under a ½-inch hem twice on one long edge of both back rectangles. Stitch ½ inch from the folded edge. Overlap the finished edges of the two rectangles and adjust to create a 25-inch square. Machine-baste ⅜ inch from the raw edges in the overlap area (Figure 4 on page 46).

25"

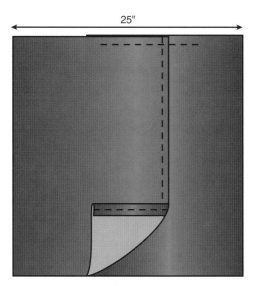

Figure 4
Lap panels and baste
overlaps together.

9. With right sides together, pin the pillow front to the pillow back. Stitch ½ inch from the raw edges. Trim the corners to reduce bulk and turn the pillow right side out. If desired, sew hook-and-loop tape to the back overlap area.

10. Insert the pillow form through the opening in the back.

Stacked & Stitched

Materials for Stacked & Stitched

- ⅞ yard 54-inch-wide black silk dupioni
- ¼ yard each 9 colors 45- or 54-inch-wide silk dupioni
- ¾ yard lightweight batting
- 3 yards ⅜-inch-diameter cord trim with lip
- 30-weight rayon embroidery thread
- All-purpose thread to match pillow fabric
- Chalk marker
- Temporary spray adhesive
- Optional: ¼ yard ½-inch-wide hook-and-loop tape
- 24-inch-square pillow form
- Optional: Polyester fiberfill
- Basic sewing tools and equipment

Cutting for Stacked & Stitched

- From the black silk, cut one 25-inch square for the pillow front and two 17 x 25-inch rectangles for the pillow back.
- From each colored silk, cut one each 6-inch-, 5-inch- and 4-inch-diameter circle.
- From the batting, cut one 25-inch square.

Assembly for Stacked & Stitched

Project Note: Use ½-inch-wide seam allowances unless otherwise directed.

1. Using the chalk marker, draw a grid on the right side of the black square for circle placement guidelines (Figure 1).

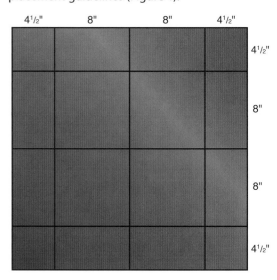

4½"   8"   8"   4½"

4½"

8"

8"

4½"

Figure 1
Draw grid on pillow front.

2. Stack the circles into nine sets of three each, mixing and matching colors for a varied arrangement. When satisfied with the color arrangement, apply a light coat of temporary spray adhesive to the wrong side of each circle and smooth into place. Be sure to center each circle as you add it to its stack.

3. Lightly fold each stack in half and then in half again and finger-press to make creases for centering purposes.

4. Apply a light coat of temporary spray adhesive to the wrong side of the circle stack. Position each stack on the pillow-cover top, matching the crease lines to the gridlines drawn earlier.

5. Chalk-mark the gridlines across the circles (Figure 2).

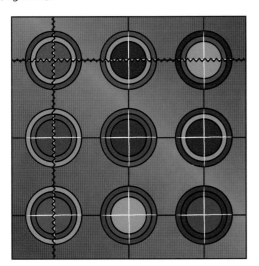

Figure 2
Redraw grid lines through circles.
Zigzag over all lines.

6. Using 30-weight rayon thread in the needle and a medium-width, medium-length zigzag stitch, zigzag over the chalked lines in both directions to hold the circles in place.

7. Place the batting square face up on a flat surface and apply a light coat of temporary adhesive. Center the pillow front on top and smooth into place. Machine-baste ⅜ inch from the raw edges.

8. Beginning at the center of one edge of the pillow top, pin the cord trim in place along the ½-inch seam line and clip the corners as needed for smoothly turned corners. Join the cord ends where they meet using one of the methods shown on page 13.

Raggedy Resistant?

• For even more raw-edge fun, cut the circles with decorative-edge scissors.

• If the idea of leaving ragged and frayed edges is not your style, consider using faux suede or felt for the colorful circles and pillow base instead of silk.

• If you love the silk, but not the raw edges, add ½ inch to each circle diameter and then cut twice as many of each circle size. Sew two (matching or contrasting) circles together with right sides facing and make a small slash in the center of the color that you want on the underside. Turn right side out and press. The slits will be hidden when the circles are stacked and stitched to the pillow top (Figure 1).

Figure 1
Sew 2 circles together. Make slit in underlayer for turning.

• If serging is your forté and you have mastered serging in circles, try finishing the circle edges with decorative serging. Use a contrasting-color thread for even more interest.

• Try stacking other shapes—squares, octagons or triangles—for a different effect.

9. Use a zipper foot to stitch close to the cord.

10. To prepare the pillow back with envelope closure, turn under and press a double ½-inch-wide hem at one long edge of each 17 x 25-inch silk panel. Stitch.

11. Lap one finished edge over the other and adjust so the resulting piece is 25 inches square. Machine-baste ⅜ inch from the raw edges in the overlap area as shown in Figure 4 for Jeweled Windows on page 46.

12. With right sides facing and the back of the pillow top facing you, pin the pillow top to the pillow back. Attach the zipper foot and adjust to the right of the needle. Adjust the needle position to the left if possible on your machine. Stitch just inside the previous stitching to sew the pieces together.

13. Clip the corners to reduce bulk and turn the pillow cover right side out. If desired, sew hook-and-loop tape fasteners to the envelope opening.

14. Insert the pillow form and if necessary, fill the corners with small handfuls of polyester fiberfill.

Tabs & Tassels

Materials for Tabs & Tassels
- 1 yard 54-inch-wide black silk dupioni or similar fabric of your choice
- ⅓ yard each of 3 colors 45-inch-wide silk dupioni
- ¼ yard each 2 additional colors 45-inch-wide silk dupioni
- ¾ yard lightweight batting
- ⅓ yard 45-inch-wide lightweight fusible interfacing
- 4 (3½-inch-long) tassels
- 1 (5-inch-long) tassel
- All-purpose thread to match fabrics
- Pattern tracing paper or cloth
- Temporary spray adhesive
- Fabric/craft glue
- 24-inch-square pillow form
- ¼ yard ½-inch-wide hook-and-loop tape (optional)
- Basic sewing tools and equipment

Cutting for Tabs & Tassels
- From the black silk dupioni, cut one 25-inch square for the pillow front and two 17 x 25-inch rectangles for the pillow back.
- Trace the full-size tab pattern on page 51 onto pattern tracing paper or cloth and cut out. Follow the directions on the pattern to enlarge it for the medium and large sizes.
- From the remaining black silk dupioni, cut one large tab, two medium tabs and two small tabs using the pattern pieces on page 51.
- From the colored silks and from the fusible interfacing, cut one large tab, two medium tabs and two small tabs.
- From silk scraps, cut five 1½ x 6-inch strips for the tassel covers.
- From the batting, cut one 26-inch square.

Assembly for Tabs & Tassels

Project Note: *Use ½-inch-wide seam allowances unless otherwise directed.*

1. Apply a light coat of temporary spray adhesive to the 26-inch batting square and center the 25-inch silk square face up on top. Smooth into place and trim the excess batting even with the edges of the square. Machine-baste ⅜ inch from the raw edges.

2. Following the manufacturer's directions, apply the interfacing pieces to the wrong side of their respective silk tabs.

3. With right sides together, sew a colored tab to a black tab. Use a ½-inch-wide seam allowance and leave the short straight end open for turning (Figure 1). Trim the seams and clip the corners. Turn right side out; press (Figure 1).

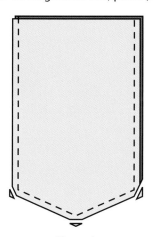

Figure 1
Stitch and trim tabs.

4. With raw edges even, position the tabs along the upper edge of the pillow front. Center the longest tab and add the remaining tabs to each side with about ¾ inch of the pillow front exposed beyond the outer edge of the outermost tabs. Stitch in place a scant ½ inch from the raw edges (Figure 2).

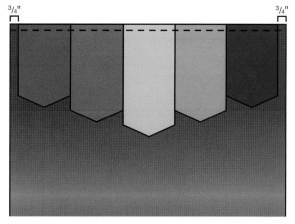

3/4"   3/4"

Figure 2
Stitch tabs to pillow front upper edge.

5. To prepare the pillow back with envelope closure, turn under and press a double ½-inch-wide hem at one long edge of each 17 x 25-inch silk panel. Stitch.

6. Lap one finished edge over the other and adjust so the resulting piece is 25 inches square. Machine-baste ⅜ inch from the raw edges in the overlap area as shown in Figure 4 for Jeweled Windows on page 46.

7. With right sides together, pin the pillow front to the pillow back. Make sure the tabs are lying smooth and flat inside the layers. Stitch. Trim the corners and turn the pillow cover right side out through the back opening. If desired, sew hook-and-loop fastener tape to the back overlap area.

8. Cut and apply a 1¼ x 6-inch strip of fusible interfacing to the wrong side of each 1½ x 6-inch silk strip. Sew the strips together using ¼-inch-wide seams. Press the seams open. Cut a 3¼-inch-wide bias piece (see Note below) from the pieced square (Figure 3 on page 50). Turn under and press ½ inch on each long edge (Figure 4 on page 50).

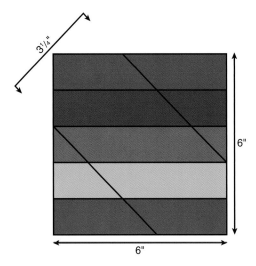

Figure 3
Sew strips together.

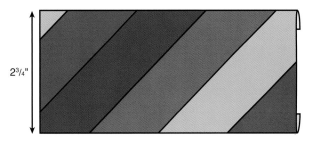

Figure 4
Turn under ¹/₂" on each long edge.

Note: Before cutting the piece, measure the tassel head of the large tassel. You may need to cut the piece wider to cover it, depending on its shape and size.

9. Wrap the tassel head with the pieced fabric and use fabric adhesive to attach the lower edge of the wrap to the head. Trim any extra fabric where the ends meet, leaving ½ inch to turn under for a neat finish. Glue or hand-sew in place (Figure 5).

Figure 5
Wrap tassel top with fabric.

10. Center and hand-sew the small tassels to the wrong side of the small and medium tabs, and the large tassel to the large tab.

11. Insert the pillow form through the opening in the pillow cover.

12. If desired, place a small dab of fabric glue under the lower edge of each tab to hold it in place on the pillow front. ◆

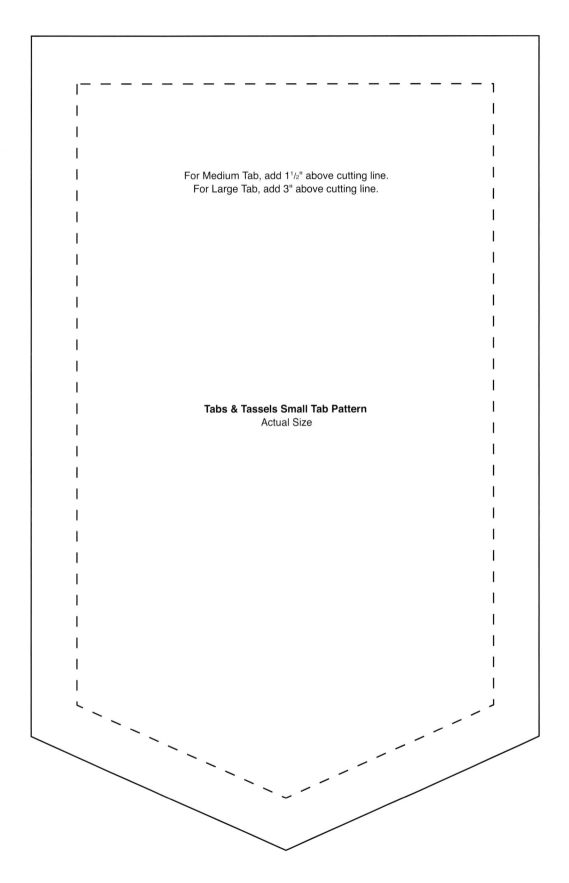

For Medium Tab, add 1¹⁄₂" above cutting line.
For Large Tab, add 3" above cutting line.

Tabs & Tassels Small Tab Pattern
Actual Size

Beautifully Enveloped

DESIGN BY LYNN WEGLARZ

Here's a pretty pillow with a split personality. Each side of the interior pillow is a different color—one gold, one red to coordinate with the colors in its silk plaid envelope. Consider using a holiday print on one side of the cover for the knife-edge pillow and a yearlong print on the other, with a solid color for the envelope. Then it's a simple matter to quick change the decorating scheme to coordinate with the holiday.

Finished Sizes
Envelope: 19½ inches square
Inner Pillow: 16 inches square

Materials
- 54-inch-wide decorator fabric
  ½ yard Fabric A for pillow front
  ½ yard Fabric B for pillow back
  ¾ yard plaid Fabric C for envelope front
  ⅝ yard Fabric D for envelope back
- 1 yard coordinating ribbon for closure
- 16-inch-square knife-edge pillow form
- All-purpose thread to match fabrics
- Fabric marking pen or dressmaker's chalk
- Optional: ¼ yard lightweight batting
- Optional: Temporary spray adhesive
- Rotary cutter, mat and ruler
- Basic sewing tools and equipment

Cutting
- From Fabric A, cut one 17-inch square for the pillow cover.
- From Fabric B, cut one 17-inch square for the back side of the pillow cover.
- From Fabric C, cut four 8½ x 17-inch rectangles for the envelope front and four 2½ x 22-inch bias strips for the envelope flange.
- From Fabric D, cut one 20-inch square for the envelope back.
- Optional: For added body in the flange strips (recommended), cut four 3 x 20-inch strips from lightweight batting.

Assembly

1. If the fabrics for the pillow cover and envelope back ravel, serge- or zigzag-finish the raw edges of each piece.

2. With right sides facing and using a ½-inch-wide seam allowance, sew the Fabric A and B 17-inch squares together, leaving a 12-inch-long opening in one edge for turning. Turn right side out and insert the pillow form. Slipstitch the opening edges together.

Note: *If you prefer, you can insert an invisible zipper for an inseam opening before sewing the two squares together. See page 16.*

3. Cut the ribbon into two equal lengths for the envelope closure. Center each piece of ribbon on one long cut edge of an 8½ x 17-inch rectangle for the envelope front. Machine-stitch and backstitch to secure the ribbon. With right sides facing, sew each ribboned rectangle to one of the remaining rectangles (Figure 1).

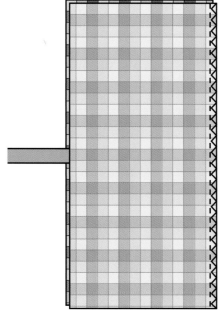

Figure 1
Sew envelope front panels
together with ribbon between.
Make 2.

Trim the seam allowance to ¼ inch and serge or zigzag the seam allowances together.

4. Turn the envelope panels right side out and press along the stitched edge. Edgestitch the seamed edge, keeping the ribbon out of the way of the stitching. Machine-baste the raw edges together around each panel (Figure 2).

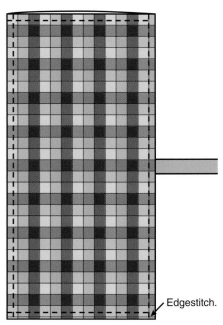

Edgestitch.

Figure 2
Turn and press panels. Machine
baste ¹/₂" from raw edges.

5. Optional: For added body, position a batting strip on the wrong side of each bias flange strip. Use temporary spray adhesive to hold the layers together or machine-baste a scant ¼ inch from the long edges. Trim the batting strips even with the flange-strip edges.

6. Place the two envelope panels face down on the right side of one bias flange strip, centering the pair on the strip. Pin in place. Beginning and ending the stitching ¼ inch from the raw edges of the panel, stitch ¼ inch from the raw edges. Repeat at the opposite edge (Figure 3).

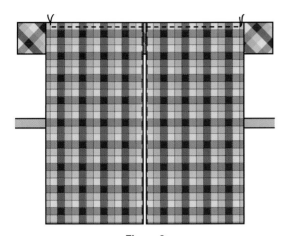

Figure 3
Stitch envelope panels to bias strip.
End stitching ¹/₄" from corners.

7. Add flange strips to the remaining raw edges of the envelope front in the same manner.

8. To complete the flange corners, fold the envelope panel in half diagonally with the flange seam line and outer raw edges aligned. Starting at the end of the stitching, draw a 45-degree-angle seam line on the flange. Pin and stitch (Figure 4). Trim the excess flange, leaving a ½-inch-wide seam. Press the seam open.

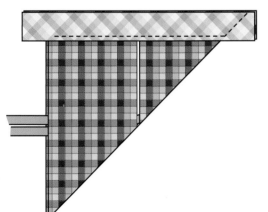

Figure 4
Stitch mitered corners in flange.

9. Repeat step 8 to complete the remaining corners. If you added batting, trim the batting close to the stitching to eliminate excess bulk. Press the seams toward the flange.

10. With raw edges even and right sides together, pin the envelope front to the back. Stitch ¼ inch from the raw edges. Zigzag or serge the seam allowances together. Turn right side out and press the outer edges.

11. Pin the envelope to the front around the flange seam. Stitch in the ditch of the seam to complete the flange (Figure 5).

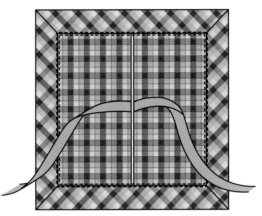

Figure 5
Stitch in the ditch along
the flange seam.

12. Insert the pillow and tie the ribbons in a neat bow. Trim the ribbon ends at a 45-degree angle. ◆

Diamond Sophisticate

DESIGN BY PAM LINDQUIST

Simple patchwork shapes strike an elegant pose when cut from silken fabrics in colors to match your decor. Add an appliqué or embroidery for even more dramatic flair.

Finished Size

18 inches square

Materials

- 54-inch-wide silk dupioni or similar synthetic fabric
    - ½ yard red for patchwork
    - 1 yard black for patchwork and pillow back
- 1½ yards 44-inch-wide lightweight knit or weft-insertion fusible interfacing
- 18-inch-long zipper
- 18-inch-square knife-edge pillow form
- All-purpose thread to match fabrics
- Rotary cutter, mat and ruler
- Zipper foot
- Basic sewing tools and equipment

Cutting

- From the red fabric, cut four 3 x 54-inch strips.
- From the black fabric, cut four 3 x 54-inch strips. From the remaining black fabric, cut one 9 x 18½-inch rectangle and one 11 x 18½-inch rectangle.
- From the fusible interfacing, cut (13) 3 x 40-inch strips, one 9½ x 18½-inch rectangle and one 11 x 18½-inch rectangle.

Assembly

***Project Note:** Use ¼-inch-wide seam allowances.*

1. Following the manufacturer's directions, apply the fusible interfacing strips to the wrong side of each 3-inch-wide fabric strip. Butt the short cut edges of the interfacing where necessary to cover each strip; trim excess. Cut an additional strip of interfacing if necessary. Apply the interfacing rectangles to the wrong side of the pillow back pieces.

2. Fold a 3-inch-wide red strip in half crosswise and make a 45-degree-angle cut as shown in Figure 1. With the strip still folded, cut eight sets of mirror-image 1⅞-inch-wide diamonds from the strip (Figure 1).

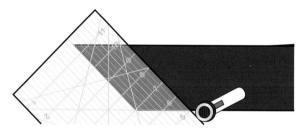

Figure 1
Fold each strip in half
and cut 45-degree-angle diamonds.

3. Repeat steps 2 and 3 with each of the remaining red and the black strips.

4. Sew the red and black diamonds together in pairs and press the seams toward the black diamond in each pair (Figure 2).

Figure 2
Sew diamonds together in pairs.

5. Arrange the diamond pairs in alternating fashion in nine rows of five diamond pairs each. Sew the diamond pairs together in rows. Press the seams toward the black diamonds (Figure 3).

Figure 3
Arrange diamond pairs in
9 rows of 5 diamond pairs each.
Sew diamond pairs together
in each row.

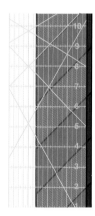

Figure 4
Trim diamond strips to 2½" wide.

6. Trim each strip to 2½ inches wide (Figure 4).

7. Pin the strips together, taking care to match the seam intersections. Stitch ¼ inch from the raw edges and press the seams in one direction. Trim the top and bottom edges evenly so the resulting square measures 18½ inches square (Figure 5).

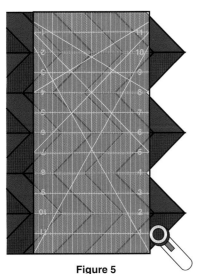

Figure 5
Trim patchwork panel
to 18½" square.

8. With right sides facing, sew the two back panels together ¾ inch from the raw edges. Stitch the first 1¼ inches with the normal stitch length and backstitch. Change to a basting length stitch for the center 16 inches; backstitch and return to the normal stitch length for the remaining 1¼ inches (Figure 6). Press the seam open.

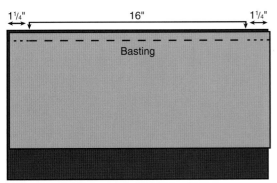

Figure 6
Prepare back panel for zipper.

9. Insert the zipper in the seam using a lapped application as shown on page 15. UNZIP THE ZIPPER.

10. With right sides together, pin the pillow top to the pillow back. Stitch ¼ inch from the raw edges, and then zigzag or serge the seam allowances together. Turn right side out.

11. Insert the pillow and zip the zipper. ◆

Added Elegance

Add an embroidered appliqué to the pillow front before sewing the pillow front and back together. Alternatively, you can embroider a favorite motif directly on the patchwork pillow front.

1. Purchase an appliqué or make one by embroidering a favorite motif on a layer of tulle or other lightweight sheer fabric.

2. Cut out around the embroidery, leaving a ¼-inch-wide turn-under allowance.

3. Pin the appliqué in place on the pillow top, tucking under the fabric allowance.

4. Machine- or hand-sew in place.

5. Complete the pillow cover following the directions above.

Road to Marrakech

DESIGN BY JANIS BULLIS

Create a beautiful pillow that would make even Moroccan royalty envious, using luscious velvet, satin and brocade ribbons in jewel tones with golden accents. Complete the look with tassels and twisted cord in coordinating colors.

Finished Size
16 inches square

Materials
- 1 yard 44- or 54-inch-wide fabric for the pillow front and back
- ½ yard medium-weight fusible interfacing
- 1 yard each 16–18 different decorative and solid-color ribbons in widths of ⅝–1 inch
- 2 yards ⅜-inch-diameter decorative cord pip
- 4 (3-inch-long) tassels in four different colors
- 1 (4-inch-long) tassel
- 1 (¾-inch-diameter) gold button for pillow center
- 16-inch-square pillow form
- All-purpose thread in colors to match fabric and ribbons
- Chalk marker
- Rotary cutter, mat and ruler
- Basic sewing tools and equipment

Cutting
- For the pillow front, cut one 17-inch square.
- Cut two 17 x 20-inch rectangles for the pillow back with envelope closure.
- Cut one 17-inch square of fusible interfacing.

Assembly

Project Notes: *Use ½-inch-wide seam allowances.*

1. Following the manufacturer's directions, apply the fusible interfacing to the wrong side of one of the fabric squares.

2. Referring to Figure 1, mark lines on the right side of the pillow top.

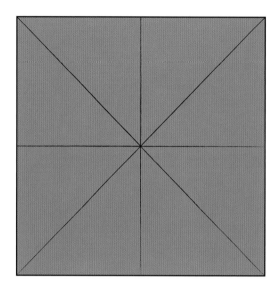

Figure 1
Draw placement
guidelines on pillow top.

3. Separate ribbons into two different assortments, dividing prints, solids and similar colors evenly. Spread each assortment out separately, in an attractive order, alternating colors, prints and widths. Cut all ribbons into ½-yard lengths.

4. Choosing from one ribbon assortment, pin a single ribbon inside the marked line of one 90-degree quadrant. Make a 45-degree-angle fold to miter the corner. Stitch the ribbon in place along both long edges, pivoting at the corners. Repeat with the identical ribbon along the opposite quadrant (Figure 2).

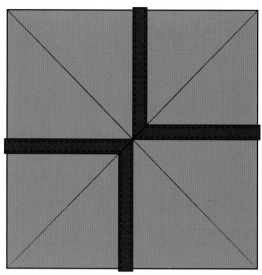

Figure 2
Position and sew ribbons
to opposite quadrants.

5. Using a second identical ribbon pair, pin and stitch them inside the same two quadrants, aligning them with the first ribbon pair. Continue to apply ribbon pairs in these two quadrants until the fabric is covered with ribbon in the two opposite quadrants (Figure 3).

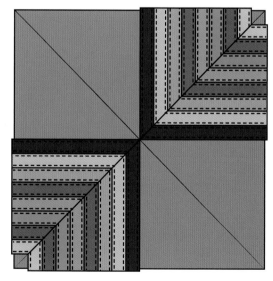

Figure 3
Add ribbons to cover quadrants.

6. Choosing from the second ribbon assortment, apply ribbon pairs to the remaining two quadrants in the same manner.

7. Beginning at the center of one edge of the beribboned pillow top, pin and stitch the cord trim to the pillow top. Begin and end the stitching a few inches short of the area where the cord ends will meet, and clip the lip of the cord to turn the corners smoothly (Figure 4).

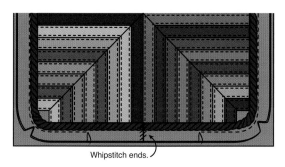

Whipstitch ends.

Figure 4
Sew cord piping to pillow-top edge,
leaving several inches unstitched at both ends.
Butt ends at center and whipstitch.

8. Cut the cord ends so they butt and whipstitch the cord ends together, but do not attach them to the pillow top yet.

9. From the pillow fabric or a fabric scrap that matches the cord trim, cut a 1½ x 2½-inch rectangle. Turn under and press ¼ inch at each long edge. Wrap the piece around the cord to camouflage the joined ends. Machine-stitch the loose, fabric-wrapped section of the cord to the pillow top (Figure 5).

Figure 5
Wrap fabric over cord ends.
Complete stitching.

10. Fold each 17 x 20-inch rectangle for the pillow back in half with wrong sides facing to create 10 x 17-inch rectangles. Press. Stitch ½ inch from the fold on each one.

11. Overlap the stitched edges of the rectangles and adjust to create a 17-inch square. Pin the layers together, and then machine-baste ⅜ inch from the raw edges in the overlap area as shown in Figure 2 on page 29.

12. With right sides facing and all raw edges even, pin and stitch the pillow top to the pillow back. Turn the pillow cover right side out.

13. Hand-tack a tassel to each corner of the pillow cover.

14. Insert the pillow through the opening in the back. Sew the button and tassel to the pillow center. For added dimension, catch the pillow in the stitching. (If you must clean the pillow cover, you will need to remove the button and tassel and sew in place when you replace the cover.) ◆

Mixed Media

DESIGN BY BARBARA WEILAND

Use this interesting pillow design as a springboard for your own creativity. Choose a printed decorator fabric panel to border with coordinating fabrics and add appliqués or embroidery for the trim. Flat piping frames one edge. Your pillow will be a one-of-a-kind creation because of your fabric choices.

Finished Size
13 x 17 inches

Materials
- 1 decorative fabric panel, 10½ x 15¾ inches (see Note at the beginning of the cutting directions)
- 3½ x 16½-inch strip coordinating print for left border
- 2¼ x 13½-inch strip coordinating fabric for bottom border
- 1 x 16-inch strip contrasting fabric scrap for the flat piping
- ½ yard coordinating fabric for pillow back
- ⅙ yard contrasting fabric for piping
- 1¾ yards ⁵⁄₃₂-inch-diameter cotton cord for piping
- 3 embroidered appliqués (purchased or make your own)
- Optional: 14 x 18-inch piece lightweight batting
- 14- or 16-inch-long zipper for back opening
- Custom-made knife-edge pillow insert (see directions on page 8)
- Zipper foot
- Rotary cutter, mat and ruler
- Basic sewing tools and equipment

Cutting
Note: *Cutting is given for the pillow shown. You may need to adjust the cutting dimensions for all pieces, depending on the printed fabric panel you wish to use for the focal point in the pillow cover. Experiment with border widths that are suitable for your panel by drawing the finished size (excluding ¼-inch-wide seam allowances all around). Then draw in borders of a pleasing width. Don't forget to add ¼ inch all around for seam allowances when cutting the pieces from the desired fabrics.*

• From the fabric for the pillow back, cut one 13½ x 18½-inch panel.
• From the fabric for the outer-edge piping, cut two 2 x 35-inch strips. Sew together with bias seams as shown on page 11 and press the seam open.

Assembly

Project Note: *Use ¼-inch-wide seam allowances.*

1. Fold the back panel as shown and press. Machine-baste ¾ inch from the pressed edge (Figure 1).

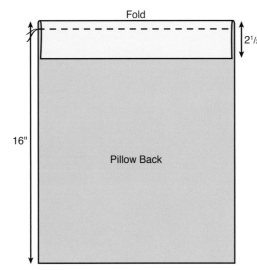

Figure 1
Fold panel and machine-baste ³/₄" from fold.

2. Slash the folded edge and press the seam open. Insert the zipper in the seam following the directions on page 15 for a lapped zipper. Note that the zipper will be too long, and make sure to follow the directions carefully for cutting the excess. The zipper opening will extend all the way across the back panel (Figure 2).

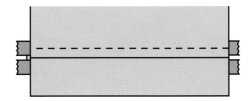

Figure 2
Excess zipper extends at each end.

3. Wrap the 2-inch-wide strip around the cotton cord to make piping as shown on page 12.

4. Refer to Figure 3 for steps 4 and 5. Fold the 1 x 16½-inch contrast strip in half lengthwise with wrong sides facing and press. Pin the flat piping strip to the left-hand long edge of the fabric panel, and stitch a scant ¼ inch from the raw edges. With right sides facing, pin the 3½ x 16-inch border strip to the left edge of the panel and stitch ¼ inch from the raw edges. Press the seam toward the center panel so the flat piping lies on top of the side border (Figure 3).

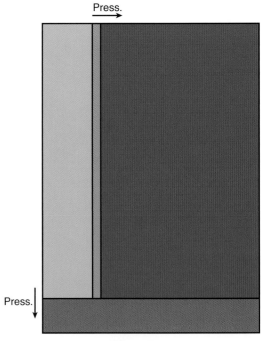

Figure 3
Sew borders to fabric panel.

5. Sew the bottom border strip to the bottom edge of the panel and press the seam toward the border.

6. Optional: Back the fabric panel with a layer of lightweight batting, and quilt around selected motifs in the print panel. Trim the batting even with the outer edges of the completed pillow front.

7. Position and stitch embroidered motifs or appliqués to the left border. To make your own embroidered appliqués, see Embroider Your Own. If desired, you may embroider motifs on the border instead of applying embroidered appliqués.

8. UNZIP THE ZIPPER. Attach the zipper foot and adjust it to the right of the needle. With right sides facing, pin the pillow back to the pillow front. Position so the zipper is toward the bottom of the pillow. With the back of the pillow front facing you, stitch just inside the piping stitching all the way around the pillow.

9. Turn the pillow cover right side out and insert the pillow form. ◆

Embroider Your Own!

You can make your own appliqués on your embroidery machine.

1. Choose a densely embroidered design.

2. Hoop a layer of polyester or nylon organza and attach the hoop to your embroidery machine.

3. Stitch out the design using rayon (not polyester) embroidery thread.

4. Use a hot stencil-cutting tool to gently cut the design away from the still-hooped fabric. Take care to avoid burning yourself. Leaving the fabric hooped makes it easier to guide the cutting tool. Unhoop and discard the remaining fabric.

Note: *You can also embroider on one or more layers of tulle and cut away in the same manner. Test first.*

Hurrah for the Red, White & Blue

DESIGNS BY KAREN DILLON

America's classic colors star in these two easy-to-stitch pillows with button detailing. Use them together in a patriotic-themed bedroom or reinterpret them in your favorite color combos to suit your decorating style.

Finished Sizes
Drumroll Please: 16 inches square
Check This Out: 16 inches square

Drumroll Please

Materials for Drumroll Please
- ½ yard red linen or linenlike fabric
- ½ yard red-and-white ticking stripe cotton or linen
- 1½ yards navy blue narrow cord
- 17-inch square lightweight batting
- 2 yards ¹⁰⁄₃₂-inch-diameter cotton cord for welting
- 8 (2-hole) ⅝-inch-diameter white buttons
- 2 (1-inch) squares hook-and-loop tape for envelope closure
- 16-inch-square knife-edge pillow form
- All-purpose thread to match and contrast with fabrics
- Zipper foot
- Rotary cutter, mat and ruler
- Basic sewing tools and equipment

Cutting for Drumroll Please

Note: *Cutting dimensions result in a pillow cover that fits snugly over the 16-inch pillow form.*

- From the red linen, cut two 5¾ x 16-inch rectangles for the pillow front and two 13 x 16-inch rectangles for the pillow back with envelope closure.
- From the ticking stripe, cut one 5½ x 16-inch strip with the stripes running along the length of the panel. From the remainder of the stripe, cut enough 2-inch-wide bias strips to make a 70-inch-long strip for the piping.

Assembly for Drumroll Please

1. Using ¼-inch-wide seam allowances, sew the red-and-white ticking and the red linen panels together for the pillow front. Serge or zigzag the seam allowances together, and then press them toward the red panels. Mark the position for the navy blue cord on the pillow front. Arrange the cord and tack in place by hand or machine (Figure 1).

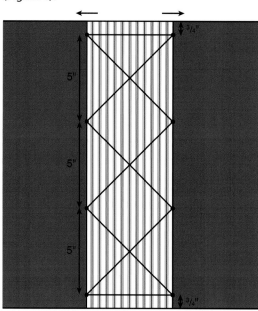

Figure 1
Sew panels together.
Tack cord in place at seams.

2. Smooth the pillow top in place on top of the batting and stitch ¼ inch from the edges. Trim the batting even with the pillow top.

3. Turn under and press 1 inch at one long edge of each 13 x 16-inch rectangle. Turn again and press to make a double-layer hem. Edgestitch along the inner fold. Position and stitch hook-and-loop tape closures to the opening edges as shown. Lap the panels and adhere the closures. The resulting panel should measure 16 inches square (Figure 2).

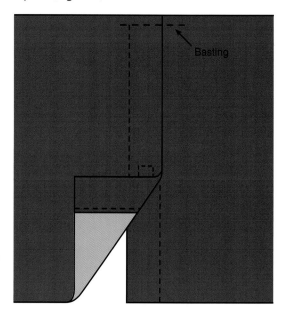

Figure 2
Overlap hemmed panels.
Add hook-and-loop closures.

4. Using bias seams, sew the striped bias strips together and press the seams open. Following the directions on page 12, use the strip and the cotton cord to create the welting for the outer edge of the pillow. If necessary, trim the welting seam allowance to ½ inch.

5. With a contrasting thread in the bobbin and the zipper foot attached and adjusted to the right of the needle, machine-baste the welting to the outer edge of the pillow top. Begin and end the welting at the center of the striped panel with a neat join as shown on page 13. Take care to keep the navy blue cord out of the way of the stitching.

6. Pin the pillow front to the pillow back panel with right sides facing and the back of the pillow top facing you so you can see the welting stitching. Stitch just inside the first stitching line as close to the cord in the welting as possible.

7. Hand-sew buttons in place at each corner of the navy blue cord.

8. Insert the pillow form through the envelope closure in the back of the pillow.

Check This Out

Materials for Check This Out
- 54-inch-wide decorator fabrics
  - ⅜ yard 1-inch blue-and-white check linen or linenlike fabric
  - ½ yard coordinating blue linen or linenlike fabric
- 1¼ yards narrow red decorative cord
- 17-inch square lightweight batting
- Air- or water-soluble marking pen
- All-purpose thread to match fabrics and red thread for tassels and buttons
- 13 (2-hole) ⅝-inch-diameter white buttons
- 4 red tassels (3½ inches long, excluding the tassel loop)
- 2 (1-inch) squares hook-and-loop tape for envelope closure
- 16-inch-square knife-edge pillow form
- Cellophane tape
- Zipper foot
- Rotary cutter, mat and ruler
- Basic sewing tools and equipment

Cutting for Check This Out
- From the check fabric, cut one 10-inch square, taking care to cut so that the ½-inch-wide seam allowances are in the white squares (Figure 1).

Figure 1
Cut front panel.

- From the blue fabric, cut four 4 x 18-inch strips for the borders and two 11½ x 16-inch rectangles for the pillow back with envelope closure.

Assembly for Check This Out

Project Note: *Use ½-inch-wide seam allowances throughout.*

1. Mark the center at each edge of the center square and at one long edge of each blue 4 x 18-inch strip.

2. Matching centers, sew a border strip to one edge of the center square. Begin and end the stitching precisely ½ inch from the corners of the square (Figure 2). Repeat with the remaining three strips.

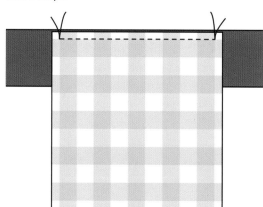

Figure 2
Stitch border strip to pillow top.
Begin and end stitching ¹/₂" from corners.

3. Refer to Figure 3 for steps 3 and 4. To complete each mitered corner in the borders, fold the pillow top in half diagonally and align the raw edges of the two facing border strips. Turn the seam allowances down toward the center square so you can see the previous stitching. Draw a diagonal line from the end of the border stitching to the outer edge. Pin. Machine-baste along the line. Open the basted corner and make sure it is true and square. Adjust as needed and stitch permanently. Remove the basting.

4. Repeat step 3 at each of the remaining corners. Trim the excess fabric at each corner,

leaving a ½-inch-wide seam allowance. Press the seams open.

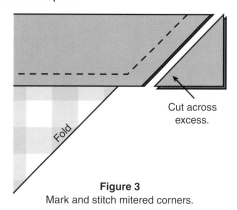

Figure 3
Mark and stitch mitered corners.

5. Center the completed pillow top face up on top of the 17-inch batting square and smooth into place. Pin. Draw diagonal lines from corner to corner across the checked pillow top center. Draw additional lines, spacing them two squares apart. Stitch on the lines and pull the thread tails through to the underside to tie off securely. Stitch in the ditch of the seam around the pillow top between the border and the center square (Figure 4).

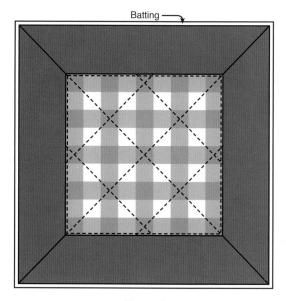

Figure 4
Quilt layers together on diagonal lines.
Stitch in the ditch around center panel.

6. From the red cord, cut four 10-inch-long strips. To prevent the cord from untwisting, wrap cellophane tape around the cord before cutting so the tape will secure both cut ends at each cut. Fold each cord in half and hand-tack at a corner of the inner seam on the pillow top.

7. Using red thread in the needle, sew a button at each point where the quilting lines intersect (Figure 5).

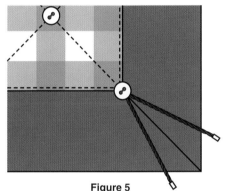

Figure 5
Tack cord at each corner.
Sew buttons in place at quilting-line
intersections and corners.

8. Twist the two halves of the cord at each button and position the cord over the mitered seam line. Tack to the seam allowance (Figure 6).

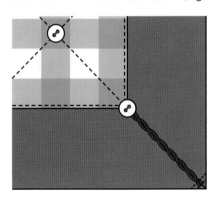

Figure 6
Twist cords together and
tack to seam allowance.

9. On one 16" edge of each of the blue rectangles for the pillow back, turn under and press ½ inch. Turn under and press an additional 1 inch and edgestitch the inner fold in place. Overlap the finished edges of the rectangles and adjust to make a 16-inch square. Sew hook-and-loop tape closures in place as shown in Figure 2 on page 70 for Drumroll Please.

10. With right sides facing, sew the pillow front and back together. At each corner, leave a small opening. Working through the back opening in the pillow cover, tuck a tassel loop through each corner opening and pin in place.

11. Attach the zipper foot and adjust to the right of the needle to complete the stitching at each corner (Figure 7). Trim the excess loop even with the seam-allowance edges.

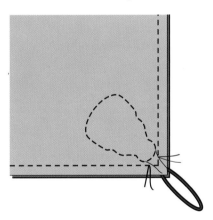

Figure 7
Pull tassels through openings.
Complete the stitching around corner.

12. Turn the pillow cover right side out and tuck the pillow form inside. ◆

Per-Sueded

DESIGN BY MARTA ALTO

Tone-on-tone embroidery and machine quilting make a rich pairing in this suede pillow.

Finished Size
14 x 18 inches

Materials
- ¾ yard 44/45-inch-wide synthetic suede
- ½ yard lightweight fusible weft-insertion or woven interfacing
- ½ yard thin cotton batting
- 16-inch zipper
- 2½ yards ¹²/₃₂-inch-diameter cotton cord for welting
- 14 x 18-inch pillow form
- All-purpose thread to match fabric
- Sewing machine with computerized embroidery unit and hoop
- Embroidery designs of your choice—one medallion-style motif and one coordinating corner motif (Embroidery Library shown)
- Rayon embroidery thread in a color that contrasts or a color that creates a tone-on-tone effect on the suede when the embroidery is stitched out
- Sticky-back embroidery stabilizer
- Temporary spray adhesive
- Chalk marker
- Optional: Polyester fiberfill
- Rotary cutter, mat and ruler
- Basic sewing tools and equipment

Cutting
- From the suede, cut one 8 x 16-inch piece for the quilted panel and set aside. Cut an 18-inch square for the pillow front; you will trim this to the correct size after completing the embroidery. From the remaining fabric, cut three 2½ x 40-inch strips for the welting and two 10 x 14-inch rectangles for the pillow back.
- From the fusible interfacing, cut one 7 x 15-inch rectangle and one 18-inch square.

Embroidery

1. Following the manufacturer's directions, apply fusible interfacing to the wrong side of the 18-inch square to stabilize it for embroidery. Repeat with the 8 x 16-inch pieces of suede and interfacing.

2. Use the chalk marker to draw a 14-inch square on the 18-inch square of suede. Also draw the center axis and diagonal lines from corner to corner (Figure 1).

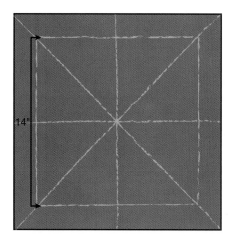

Figure 1
Chalk-mark a 14" square and
straight and diagonal lines.

3. Choose the center embroidery design in your design software and adjust the size if necessary so that it measures approximately 5–5½ inches square. Alternatively, adjust the size in the embroidery unit.

4. Hoop the stabilizer with the protective paper facing up. Score the stabilizer with a pin or needle and lift to expose the sticky surface.

5. Smooth the suede square on the stabilizer, using the chalk marks as your guide to center it in the hoop.

6. Embroider the center design. Cut jump threads and clip threads close to the surface before removing the hoop. Steam-press from the wrong side.

7. Chalk-mark the corners of a 9-inch square outside the embroidered design in the center of the square (Figure 2).

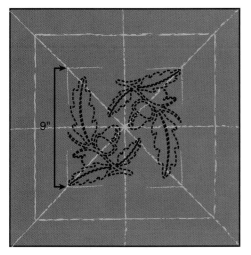

Figure 2
Chalk-mark the corners of a 9" square
with embroidered motif centered.

8. Hoop sticky-back stabilizer and embroider each corner motif. Adjust the hoop positioning as needed to center the needle over the design-centering marks before embroidering.

Note: If you have design software and a large hoop, you may be able to combine two motifs by making a mirror image of one and then spacing them the appropriate distance apart so that you only need to hoop the fabric twice to complete the corner embroideries, two sets at a time.

9. Trim the fabric to a 14-inch square, centering the design carefully so the corner designs are equidistant from the outer edges and the center motif remains centered.

Assembly

1. Use temporary spray adhesive to apply the suede to an 8 x 16-inch piece of batting.

2. Chalk-mark a 1-inch diagonal grid on the suede surface and stitch on all grid lines using the same thread you used for the embroidery. Trim the quilted panel to 7 x 15 inches (Figure 3).

Figure 3
Trim quilted panel to 7" x 15".

3. Using a bias, raw-edge seam (Figure 4), sew two of the 2½-inch-wide strips together. Cut a 70-inch length from the long piece. From the remaining strip, cut one 20-inch-long piece.

Figure 4
Bias raw-edge seam.

4. Apply a light coat of spray adhesive to the wrong side of the 20-inch length of fabric. Place a 21-inch length of the cotton cord on the adhesive, centering it in the strip. Wrap the fabric around the strip and finger-press the raw edges together. This method keeps the fabric layers from scooting and creating puckers and wrinkles in the finished welting.

5. Attach the zipper foot and adjust to the right of the needle. Stitch as close as you can to the cord to create the finished welting for the pillow interior.

6. Use the long strip to make welting for the outer edge of the pillow in the same manner.

7. Position the short piece of welting on the right side of the quilted panel at one long edge and stitch in place, stitching as close to the cord as possible. Trim the excess welting even with the panel edges.

8. Use temporary spray adhesive to attach a 14-inch square of batting to the wrong side of the embroidered suede square.

9. With right sides together and the quilted panel on top, sew the quilted panel to the left-hand edge of the embroidered panel. Stitch just inside the welting stitching for a snug fit. Finger-press the seam toward the embroidered panel (Figure 5).

10. To apply the welting to the outer edge, begin toward the center of one short edge of the completed pillow top and stitch in place with the zipper foot. Clip the welting seam allowance when you reach the corners for a smoothly rounded turn. Make a neat join where the two ends of the welting meet (see page 13).

11. Apply a lapped zipper.

12. UNZIP THE ZIPPER. With right sides facing and wrong side of the pillow top facing you, sew the pillow top to the pillow back. Use the zipper foot and stitch just inside the welting stitching for a snug fit.

13. Turn the pillow cover right side out through the zipper. Insert the pillow form and coax the pillow corners into the cover corners. Tuck bits of polyester fiberfill into each corner as needed to fill them out (see page 20). ◆

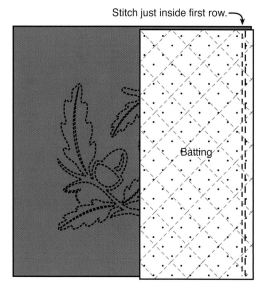

Stitch just inside first row.

Batting

Figure 5
Sew pillow front panels together.

Shapely Options

Not every pillow is a square or a rectangle. Pillows made in the round, as bolsters or neckrolls, and in other shapes add visual interest to a group of more tailored shapes. Try these interesting pillows for size and shape in your own color and fabric choices to plan a pillow grouping.

Gypsy's Dream

DESIGN BY PAM LINDQUIST

Rich colors and luxurious fabrics swirl like a gypsy's skirt on the surface of this pillow. Choose scraps of brocade, satin and velvet for this ornate pillow. In reds and greens, it would make a wonderful room accent for the Christmas season.

Finished Size

12 inches in diameter x 2½ inches thick

Materials

- Assorted wide ribbons, designer silks, taffetas, brocades, etc., to total approximately ⅝ yard for the pieced pillow front
- 13-inch square luxury fabric for the pillow back
- ¼ yard fabric for boxed edge
- 2½ yards fine gold metallic piping for outer-edge finish on boxing strip
- 1 yard muslin for pillow insert
- ⅜ yard medium-weight fusible interfacing
- 13-inch square quilt batting
- 13-inch square tissue or pattern tracing paper
- Polyester fiberfill for pillow stuffing
- 2 (2-inch diameter) covered-button forms
- Fringe tassel, about 3 inches long, excluding tassel loop
- All-purpose thread to match fabrics
- Permanent marking pen
- Decorative thread for edge finishing on the boxing strip
- Buttonhole twist or carpet thread
- Hand-sewing needle
- Zipper foot
- Rotary cutter, mat and ruler
- Basic sewing tools and equipment

Cutting

- From the assorted ribbons and fabrics for the pillow top, cut (27) 3 x 8-inch rectangles.
- From the pillow back fabric, cut one 13-inch-diameter circle.
- From the fabric for the boxing strip, cut one 3½ x 42-inch boxing strip. Repeat with the fusible interfacing.
- From the muslin, cut three 13-inch-diameter circles, four 10-inch squares and one 3½ x 42-inch boxing strip.

Assembly

Project Note: *All measurements include ½-inch-wide seam allowances unless otherwise noted.*

1. Make a pattern for a 12½-inch circle on the tissue or pattern tracing paper.

2. On the paper circle, mark the exact center with two perpendicular lines that intersect in the center. Use a sharp pencil and ruler to measure and mark an assortment of 1, 1½, 2 or 2½-inch increments around the outer edge of the paper circle in each quadrant. The quadrants may have the same increments for the wedges or different ones for a more random crazy-patch look. Draw seam lines from the outer edge to the circle center (Figure 1). If desired, plan fabric and color placements for each wedge and mark on the paper pattern. Cut the marked circle into four quarters along the quadrant lines.

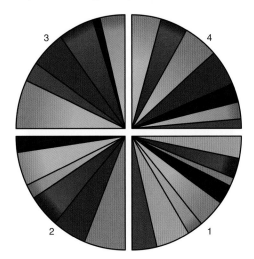

Figure 1
Draw paper pattern. Color or label
for fabric placement. Cut into quadrants.

3. Trace around each quadrant shape on a 10-inch square of muslin and transfer the seam lines with the permanent marking pen. Turn the quadrants over and if you cannot clearly see the wedge seam lines on the wrong side, darken the lines on the wrong side of the muslin

(Figure 2). On the right side, add ½-inch seam allowances to all edges.

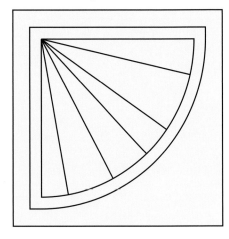

Figure 2
Trace each quadrant on muslin
square. Transfer wedge seam lines.
Add ¹/₂" seam allowance all around.

4. Choose a 3 x 8-inch rectangle for the center-most wedge on one of the muslin pieces and position it on top of the muslin. It should cover the wedge lines and cover the seam allowance at the outer curved edge. Pin in place (Figure 3). Flip the muslin over and machine-baste along the seam lines at both edges of the wedge (Figure 4).

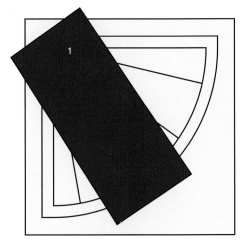

Figure 3
Position first piece of
fabric on quadrant.

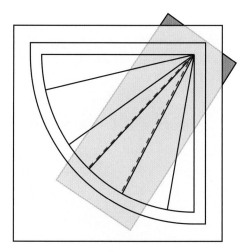

Figure 4
Machine-baste on lines
of fabric-covered wedgey

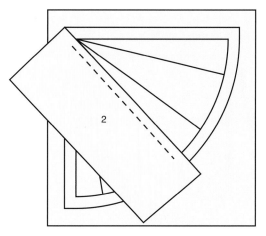

Figure 6
Trim excess fabric,
leaving ¹/₄" seam allowance.

5. Choose the next fabric rectangle; place it right side down on the first rectangle and pin in place as shown so that at least ¼ inch of the new fabric extends past the basting line. Pin in place, flip to the wrong side of the muslin and stitch on the seam line (Figure 5). On the right side, trim the excess fabric, leaving a ¼-inch-wide seam allowance (Figure 6).

6. Flip the new fabric onto the muslin and finger-press. Pin in place, flip and machine-baste to mark the next seam line (Figure 7).

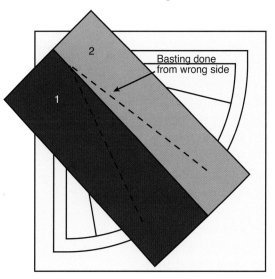

Figure 7
Flip strip 2 onto muslin. Baste
in place on wrong side of muslin.

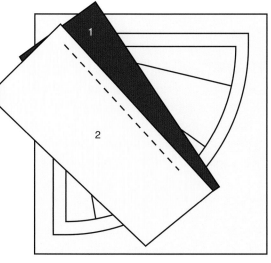

Figure 5
Sew next fabric in place
with at least ¹/₄" extending
beyond basting on strip 1.

7. Continue adding fabrics, pinning, basting and stitching in the same manner until the quadrant is covered with fabric wedges. Pin the tissue quadrant to the pieced fabric quadrant, aligning seam lines; set aside. Add fabrics to the remaining three quadrants in the same manner and pin the paper patterns in place on each one.

8. Trim each quadrant even with the paper patterns. (Figure 8).

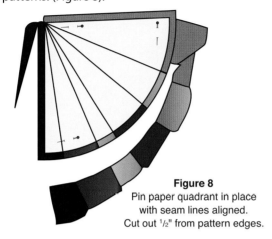

Figure 8
Pin paper quadrant in place
with seam lines aligned.
Cut out ½" from pattern edges.

9. Sew the quadrants together in pairs, using ½-inch-wide seam allowances. Trim the seams to ¼ inch and press to one side. Sew the half-circles together to complete the pillow top.

10. Following the manufacturer's directions, apply fusible interfacing to the wrong side of the boxing strip. Pin and sew piping to the right side along both edges of the boxing strip. Position so the finished width between the piping will be 2½ inches. Use the zipper foot to stitch close to the piping cord (Figure 9).

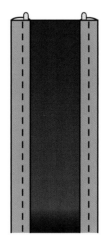

Figure 9
Sew gold piping to long
edges of boxing strip.

11. With right sides facing, pin one edge of the boxing strip to the pieced fabric circle. Mark the strip where the short ends meet for the seam line. Unpin enough of the strip so you can sew the short ends together and trim the excess, leaving a ¼-inch-wide seam allowance to press open. Re-pin the strip to the circle and stitch

with the boxing strip facing you so you can see the previous piping stitching. Stitch just inside the previous stitching (Figure 10).

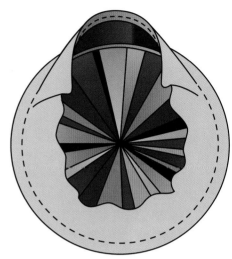

Figure 10
Sew boxing strip to pillow front.

12. Pin and sew the pillow back to the remaining edge of the boxing strip, but leave an 8-inch-long opening for inserting the pillow form.

13. Use the remaining muslin boxing strip and muslin circles to make the pillow insert, leaving an opening in one seam for stuffing. Turn right side out.

14. Stuff the insert with polyester fiberfill to the desired firmness. Turn the opening raw edges in and slipstitch or machine-stitch together.

15. Insert the pillow through the opening in the pillow cover and slipstitch the opening closed.

16. Sew the tassel loop to the center of the pillow.

17. Cover the button forms with scraps of the desired fabric following the package directions. Sew buttons to the front and back as directed in steps 8-10 on page 93. ◆

Vintage Pleats

DESIGN BY JANIS BULLIS

Combine solids and vintage-look printed fabrics to make a box cushion for extra seating or an accent pillow on a bed or wicker settee. Pleat the ruffle with the ruffler attachment for your machine or on the Clotilde's Perfect Pleater.

Finished Size
14 x 14 x 2 inches, excluding the width of
    the ruffles

Materials
- ½ yard medium-weight cotton print for pillow
    front and back
- ½ yard medium-weight cotton print coordinate
    for boxing strip
- ½ yard lightweight solid cotton for piping
- 1 yard medium-weight cotton solid for ruffle
- 2 (20-inch) squares lightweight quilt batting
- 4 yards $^6\!/_{32}$-inch cotton cord for piping filler
- 14-inch-long zipper
- 8 (1⅛-inch-diameter) covered-button forms
- 14 x 14 x 2-inch pillow foam pillow form
- All-purpose thread to match fabrics
- Heavy-duty button and carpet thread
- Dollmaker's needle
- Air-soluble fabric marker
- Zipper foot
- Ruffler attachment or Perfect Pleater
- Optional: Self-adhesive basting tape
- Rotary cutter, mat and ruler
- Basic sewing tools and equipment

Cutting
- From the print for the pillow front and back, cut
    two 15-inch squares.
- From the print coordinate for the boxing strip,
    cut one 4 x 43-inch strip and two 2½ x 15-inch
    strips for the zippered boxing panel.
- From the piping fabric, cut six true-bias strips,
    1⅝ inches wide. Sew together in sets of three
    to make two long strips; press the
    seams open.
- From the ruffle fabric, cut nine 3 x 42-inch strips.

Assembly

Project Note: Use ½-inch-wide seam allowances.

1. Cut two 65-inch pieces of cotton cord. Use the cord and the two long bias strips to make two lengths of piping as directed in Making Fabric-Covered Welting on page 12.

2. Beginning at the center of one edge on one of the pillow squares, pin piping in place. Clip the seam allowance at the corner as shown on page 12 for a smooth turn. Make a neat join when you reach the beginning point as shown on page 13. Stitch in place using the zipper foot adjusted to the right of the needle. Repeat with the remaining pillow square and piping strip.

3. Using bias seams as shown on page 11, sew the 3-inch-wide ruffle strips together. Press the seams open. Fold the strip in half lengthwise with wrong sides facing and raw edges even. Press. Cut into two equal lengths.

4. Read through Ruffler Success on page 83 now. See Note below if you do not have a ruffler. Attach the ruffler to the sewing machine following the package directions. Adjust the stitch length to average and the ruffler setting to 6 stitches per pleat. Feed the raw edges of one ruffle strip into the ruffler and stitch to create the pleats. Press the stitched edge to flatten the pleats. Repeat with the remaining ruffle strip.

Note: If you do not have a ruffler, pleat the strip using the Clotilde Perfect Pleater available from www.clotilde.com. If you prefer a gathered ruffle, machine-baste ¼ and ½ inch from the raw edge and draw up the basting to fit the pillow squares. Distribute the gathers evenly.

5. Pin the pleated ruffle to the right side of one pillow square on top of the piping with all raw edges even. Using the zipper foot, sew the ruffle in place beginning and ending the stitching a few inches shy of each cut end (Figure 1). To join the ends, mark a seam line on both ends where they meet. Pin the pleats in place at each cut end of the ruffle and then undo just enough of the stitches to allow you to sew the ruffle ends together. Trim the seam allowance to ¼ inch and press open. Pin and stitch the remainder of the ruffle in place.

Figure 1
Sew ruffle to pillow top.

6. Repeat steps 5 and 6 with the remaining square and ruffle.

7. With right sides facing, machine-baste the two short boxing strips together along the long edges. Press the seam open. Center the zipper over the seam line and baste in place by hand or with self-adhesive basting tape. On the right side, topstitch the zipper in place ¼ inch from the seam on both sides; remove the basting (Figure 2). Pin the short ends of the zippered boxing strip to the short ends of the long boxing strip. Sew the short ends together and press the seams open.

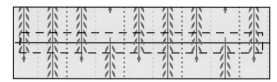

Figure 2
Insert zipper in short boxing strips.

8. Beginning at the center of the zipper panel, measure and mark both edges of the boxing strip in 7-inch increments. This marks corners and centers of the strip. Mark the center at each outer edge of each pillow square (Figure 3).

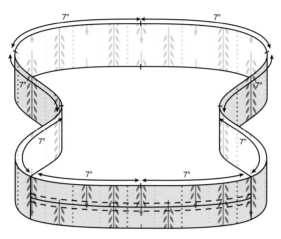

Figure 3
Mark boxing strip in 7" increments.

9. With centers matching, pin a boxing strip to one pillow square. With the square on top and the zipper foot adjusted to the right of the needle, stitch just inside the piping and ruffle stitching.

10. UNZIP the zipper. Pin and sew the remaining pillow square to the raw edge of the boxing strip. Turn the pillow cover right side out.

11. Cover pillow form with quilt batting, overlapping and hand-basting the cut edges together at the center of the sides. Trim batting at corners to keep a smooth profile (Figure 4).

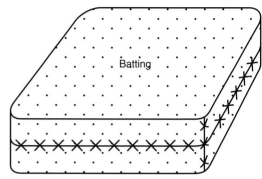

Figure 4
Wrap cushion in batting;
catchstitch edges together.

12. Insert the covered form into the pillow cover and zip the zipper. Adjust the seams so they follow the cushion edges. For easy insertion, wrap a plastic dry-cleaner bag around the covered form before inserting it in the pillow body. Rip or cut the bag so you can pull it out leaving the pillow form inside the cover.

13. Follow the package directions to cover the button forms with scraps of the ruffle fabric. On each side of the pillow, mark the button positions 4½ inches from each seam line.

14. Thread the dollmaker's needle with the heavy-duty thread and sew the buttons in place as directed in steps 8 to 10 on page 93. ◆

Ruffler Success

The ruffler attachment is a tremendous timesaver and very easy to use. High-quality rufflers are now available for many sewing machine brands and models. A generic model is also available.

• The ruffler attaches to the ankle of the machine; a double prong captures the needle bar so when you sew, the ruffler mechanism moves with the up-and-down action of the needle to grab and kick extra fabric under the needle to create pleats.

• If you press the "ruffled" fabric after stitching it, the results are perfectly spaced narrow knife pleats. Left unpressed, the pleats are a bit more like gathers.

• The ruffler has a dial that controls the fullness and look of the finished strip—play with it on your own and make samples to determine the look you want for other projects.

• Instead of placing the fabric directly on the throat plate, you must feed the fabric through the toothed blades in the front of the attachment and pull from the back to tuck it under and extend it out the back of the attachment about an inch before you begin to sew.

Note: *Do not pull the fabric toward you—the teeth of the feeder blades will catch and rip the fabric.*

• To see the results you can achieve with the ruffler, lift the pleat indicator at the front of the attachment and drop it into place in the No. 1 slot. Stitch for several inches along a ruffle strip, noticing how the blades kick in a pleat every time you take a stitch. This creates densely packed ruffles. Stop and adjust the position to No. 6. Continue stitching and notice that a ruffle is created after every six stitches. Stop again and adjust the setting to No. 12. The resulting ruffle will be less full.

• You can also adjust the distance between pleats by increasing or decreasing the sewing machine stitch length. A short sewing machine stitch length might not be acceptable for a No. 1 setting because the fabric may pile up too quickly. The resulting ruffle will be too dense, particularly on heavier fabrics. A long stitch with setting No. 6 or No. 12 will result in a ruffle that's flatter than you want. Play with the settings and the stitch lengths to determine what is best for your fabric and the desired results.

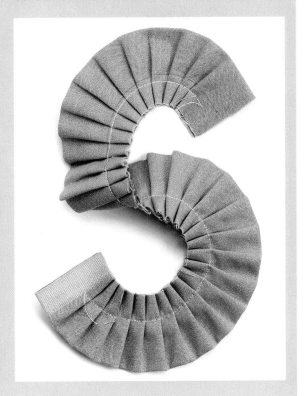

Ships Ahoy

DESIGN BY STEPHANIE CORINA GODDARD

Whether on land or at sea, bright primary colors and knotted rope evoke a nautical mood. Sail away, if only from the comfort of your armchair.

Finished Size
17 x 15 x 3 inches

Materials
- 44/45-inch-wide cotton fabric
    - ⅞ yard print with navy blue background for pillow front, back and sides
    - ¼ yard each red, yellow and blue print for the "flags"
- 1¾ yards ⅝-inch-wide navy blue grosgrain ribbon
- 5 yards ¼-inch-diameter cotton cord
- All-purpose thread to match fabrics
- Pattern tracing paper or cloth
- 14-inch-long invisible zipper
- 6 (2-hole) white star buttons, 1 inch across from point to point
- 1 (2-hole) red star button, 2 inches across from point to point
- 18 x 18 x 3-inch NU-Foam polyester cushion
- Fabric marking pen
- Rotary cutter, mat and ruler
- Serrated bread knife
- Basic sewing tools and equipment

Cutting
- Referring to Figure 1 on page 89, enlarge the pattern pieces for the pillow back, front wedge and flag on pattern tracing paper or cloth. Cut out.
- From the navy blue background print, cut two pillow backs, six wedges, and two strips each 4 x 27⅝ inches for the boxing strip.
- From each of the three prints, cut two flags.

Assembly

Project Note: *Use ½-inch-wide seam allowances unless otherwise directed.*

1. With right sides together, fold each flag in half and stitch as shown in Figure 2. Clip the corner.

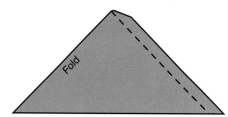

Figure 2
Fold and stitch each flag.

2. Turn each flag right side out and press. Trim the seam-allowance "ear" even with the raw edges (Figure 3).

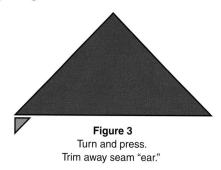

Figure 3
Turn and press.
Trim away seam "ear."

3. Center the raw edge of each flag on a front wedge and pin in place. Machine-baste ¼ inch from the raw edges (Figure 4).

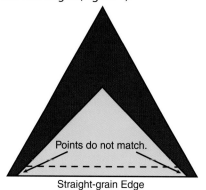

Points do not match.

Straight-grain Edge

Figure 4
Center the raw edge of each flag
over the on-grain edge of a front wedge.

4. Referring to Figure 5, arrange the wedges and sew together in sets of three. Press the seam allowances toward the point of the flag in the next wedge.

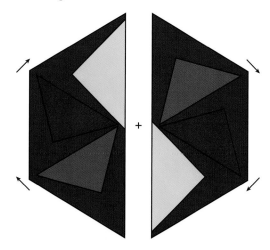

Figure 5
Sew wedges together in sets of three.
Press seams toward flag points.

5. Stitch the resulting pieces together and press the seam toward the point of the flag in the adjacent wedge. This means you will need to twist half of the center seam in the opposite direction to distribute the bulk smoothly along the center seam line.

6. At each of the six points on the pillow front, mark the ½-inch seam line (Figure 6).

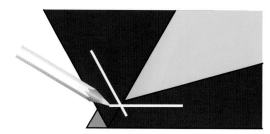

Figure 6
Mark ¹/₂" seam lines at each corner.

7. Turn under and press ½ inch on the long edge of each pillow back to mark the placement line for the invisible zipper. Open out the pressed edges and insert the invisible zipper following the directions on page 17, centering the zipper in the seam. Complete the seam above and below the top and bottom ends of the zipper.

8. Cut (24) 2½-inch-long pieces from the ⅝-inch-wide ribbon. Fold each piece in half and position two at each wedge point, spacing the inner edges of the pair of loops 1 inch apart. Pin in place and then machine-baste a scant ½ inch from the raw edges around each point, beginning and ending the stitching a few stitches past each loop edge (Figure 7). Repeat on the pillow back.

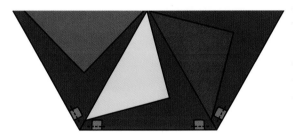

Figure 7
Sew ribbon loops ¹/₂" from
each wedge seam liney

9. Sew a star button at the point of each flag, stitching through the flag and the pillow top. Sew the large red star in place at the center of the pillow top.

10. Position the completed pillow back face up on the foam and use a marking pen to mark the shape on the foam. Draw a cutting line inside and ¼ inch from the first line (Figure 8).

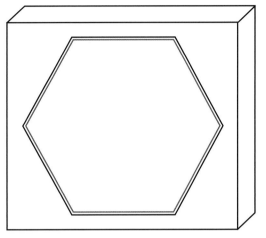

Figure 8
Trace pillowback on foamyDraw
cutting line (blue) ¹/₄" inside outliney

11. Using small sharp-pointed scissors, make a slash through the upper layer of the foam along the inner lines. Working over a protected work surface, set the blade of a serrated bread knife in the slash and, keeping the knife blade at right angles, saw straight down through the depth of the cushion. Set the pillow back and cushion aside. (The cushion will be slightly larger than the pillow cover after you sew the pieces together, but this ensures a snug fit.)

12. With right sides facing, sew the two 4-inch-wide strips together at each short end to form a ring for the boxing strip. With right sides facing and the pillow top uppermost, align the seams in the boxing strip with the opposite corners of the pillow front. Pin the remainder of the boxing strip to the outer edge of the pillow top. If necessary, clip the boxing strip to help turn a smooth corner at each pivot point.

Note: *If the boxing strip is too large, take slightly deeper seams in the strip, and then re-pin it in place. If it's too small, take slightly narrower seams and re-pin.*

13. Stitch the boxing strip to the pillow front ½ inch from the raw edges.

14. UNZIP THE ZIPPER in the pillow back. Pin and sew the pillow back to the remaining raw edge of the boxing strip as you did for the pillow front. Turn the pillow cover right side out and insert the pillow form. Adjust the form so the seam lines lie along the cushion edges.

15. Cut the cotton cord into four equal lengths and set one pair aside. Tie an overhand knot in one end of each of two remaining lengths. Tie the pieces together with a square knot (Figure 9).

Figure 9
Knot cord.

16. With the square knot centered at one wedge on the pillow top, thread the free ends of the cord through the ribbon loops and tie in a square knot where they meet on the opposite side. Tie overhand knots in the cord ends and trim excess cord. Repeat with the remaining pieces of cord and the remaining set of loops around the pillow back. ◆

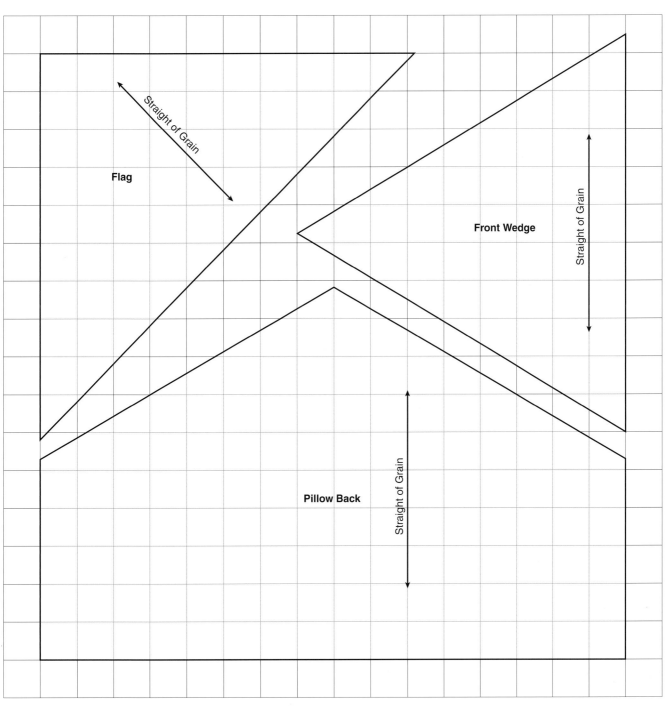

Figure 1
Patterns for Ships Ahoy
1 square = 1"

Flag

Front Wedge

Pillow Back

Straight of Grain

Eight Is Enough

DESIGN BY BARBARA WEILAND

Eight is enough for any pillow or cushion—eight corners that is! This fun shape is deceivingly simple to sew. Just cut two squares and follow the steps below. Try combining two different fabrics for a different look. Two large buttons make this a tufted cushion. Tassels are optional.

Finished Size
15 inches across, point to point

Materials
• 2 (17-inch) squares decorator fabric
• 2 large shank-style buttons, at least 1 inch
  in diameter
• All-purpose thread to match fabric
• Approximately 14 ounces polyester fiberfill
• Chopstick
• Air-soluble marking pen
• Long, large-eyed upholstery needle
• Gimp or polyester buttonhole twist or
  carpet thread
• Basic sewing tools and equipment

Assembly

Project Note: *All seam allowances are ½ inch wide.*

1. Machine-baste ½ inch from all four edges of each square. Fold each square in half and then in half again, and make ⅛-inch-long snips at the folds to mark the center of each edge. Unfold (Figure 1).

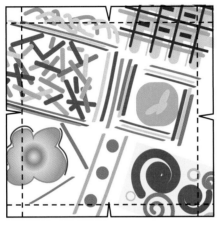

Figure 1
Machine-baste ¹/₂" from each edge of
each square. Mark centers on
each side and clip to stitching.

2. With right sides together, position one square on top of the other with the seam line at the corner of the top square at a snip mark on the bottom square. Align the snip mark on the top square with the seam line at the lower corner of the bottom square. Stitch from the seam line on the top square to the seam line on the bottom square. Backstitch carefully at the beginning and end of the seam. Make sure that the stitches do not pass the seam lines, and then carefully clip to but not past the stitching at the end of the short seam (Figure 2). Remove from the machine.

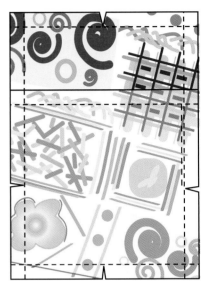

Figure 2
Stitch squares together, begining at
seam line on top square and ending
at seam line on bottom square.

3. Turn the piece over and then pin and stitch the next side of the top square to the bottom square, matching snips and seam lines as for the first seam (Figure 3).

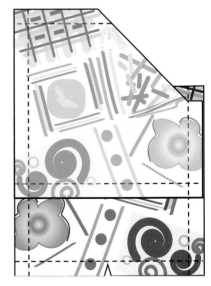

Figure 3
Stitch second side from
corner to next seam line/clip.

4. Continue in this manner until you reach the last seam. Stitch only a few inches at the beginning and end of the last seam to leave a 6-inch opening in the center.

5. Turn the cushion cover right side out. Turn under the seam allowance on one of the opening edges; press. Firmly stuff the cushion with polyester fiberfill, working it into each of the eight corners first. Use the chopstick to poke it into the corners.

6. When the pillow is completely stuffed, use doubled thread to invisibly sew the opening edges together with tiny slipstitches.

7. On the top and bottom of the eight-cornered pillow, measure and mark the center with an air-soluble marking pen.

8. Cut an 18-inch-long piece of gimp, carpet thread or buttonhole twist and slip it through the shank of one button. Tie the threads in a secure knot (Figure 4).

Figure 4
Knot gimp or buttonhole
twist around button shank.

9. Thread one end of the thread into the upholstery needle. Center the button on one side of the cushion and draw the needle through to the other side of the cushion. Remove the needle and repeat with the remaining thread end so that both ends are on the opposite side close to the center mark.

10. Pull the thread ends through the shank of the remaining button from opposite directions, and then pull them tightly to compact the center of the cushion as desired. Knot the thread ends securely under the button. ◆

Pillow Play!

• Experiment with this shape using different fabrics and trims.

• Try this pillow in smaller or larger sizes—just change the size of the square.

• Try using squares cut from two different fabrics for an interesting effect. Try a napped fabric like velveteen to create shaded variations as you turn the corners.

• Sew contrast piping to one of the two squares before assembling the cover so the seam lines have a strong outline.

• Add a tassel to each of the four corners on the top of the finished pillow. Securely and invisibly sew them in place. Tuck and tack the loops behind the tassel heads.

Tutti Frutti

DESIGN BY BARBARA WEILAND

Raw-edge bias strips stitched to a grid and overlaid on silk or linen create a textural surface for these pillow shapes. Shirring and piping accent the edges of the round cushion. Strips in the center panel of the neck roll are outlined with fringe trim.

Finished Size
Tutti Frutti Round: 12 inches in diameter,
   3 inches thick
Tutti Fruitti Roll: 9 x 14 roll

Tutti Frutti Round

Materials for Tutti Frutti Round
- 1 yard 54-inch-wide drapery sheer with burnout design for pillow front and back
- ½ yard coordinating solid-color silk dupioni or suiting or lightweight linen for the pillow front and back underlayers
- ¼ yard 44/45-inch-wide lightweight contrast fabric for shirred boxing strip and piping
- 2¼ yards ⁵⁄₃₂-inch-diameter cotton cord for piping
- 12-inch-diameter, 3-inch-thick foam pillow insert
- Sew Like Knitting sewing grid tissue (1¼-inch-grid) *or* tear-away stabilizer and fine-point permanent marking pen
- Temporary spray adhesive
- All-purpose thread to match fabrics
- Rotary cutter, mat and ruler
- Zipper foot
- Optional: Open-toe embroidery foot
- Optional: Needle-nose tweezers
- Basic sewing tools and equipment

Cutting for Tutti Frutti Round
- From the drapery sheer, cut one 14-inch square and set aside for the pillow back. From the remaining fabric, cut ¾-inch-wide bias strips, cutting them as long as possible. You will need about 46 strips that are at least 16 inches long. Stack the strips in pairs and place on a tray or cookie sheet. Cut additional strips if needed when sewing them to the grid as directed.
- From the coordinating fabric for the pillow front and back, cut two 14-inch squares.
- From the contrast fabric for the shirred boxing and piping, cut two 4 x 44-inch strips and two 2 x 44-inch strips.

Assembly for Tutti Frutti Round

Project Note: *Use ½-inch-wide seam allowances unless otherwise directed.*

1. Cut a 16-square piece of Sew Like Knitting sewing grid (1¼-inch squares) or draw a 16-square grid of 1¼-inch squares on tear-away stabilizer, using a ruler and fine-tip permanent marker.

2. Adjust the sewing machine stitch length to 15 stitches per inch. Attach an open-toe embroidery presser foot if available.

3. Center a pair of bias strips over the first grid line at the right-hand edge of the tissue and stitch in place to attach it to the grid. Sew a pair of bias strips to each of the remaining grid lines parallel to the first (Figure 1).

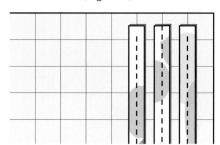

Figure 1
Sew strip pairs to
each vertical grid line.

4. Rotate the grid and sew a pair of strips to each of the grid lines, crossing the first strips you stitched to the tissue (Figure 2).

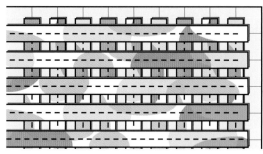

Figure 2
Overlay strip pairs across first
strips and stitch to grid lines.

5. Turn the strip-filled grid over and tug gently to help break the tissue or stabilizer away from the stitches. Remove all of the tissue from the fabric-strip lattice; use a needle-nose tweezers if necessary to remove tissue trapped under the stitches.

6. Apply a light coat of temporary spray adhesive to the right side of one of the 14-inch contrasting fabric squares. Position the fabric lattice on top and use a clear ruler to adjust as needed so the grid is square and true. Machine stitch on top of the previous stitching on the upper layer of strips to attach the lattice to the underlayer.

7. Use a light coat of temporary spray adhesive to apply the drapery sheer square to the right side of the remaining fabric square. From the lattice square and the drapery square, cut a 13-inch-diameter circle. Machine-baste a scant ½ inch from the outer edge of each circle.

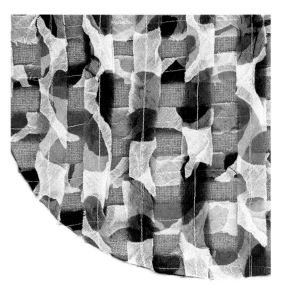

8. Using the cotton cord and the 2 x 44-inch contrast strips, make two lengths of piping as directed for Making Fabric-Covered Welting on page 12. Trim the piping seam allowance to ½ inch if necessary.

9. Sew the two 4 x 44-inch contrast strips together at one set of short ends to make one long strip. Use a ¼-inch-wide seam allowance and press the seams open.

10. Adjust the sewing machine for a basting-length stitch and machine-baste ⅝ and ⅜ inch from the long raw edges of the strip.

11. Fold the strip in half crosswise and mark both cut edges at the fold to denote the centers.

12. Draw up the basting on both long edges of the strip to create a 40-inch-long shirred boxing strip. Tie off the threads to secure the gathers. Adjust the gathers evenly along the length of the strips (Figure 3). Gently tug the strip from raw edge to raw edge to straighten out the shirring. Adjust so the shirring folds are straight and perpendicular to the long edges.

Figure 3
Draw up gathers to
create 40"-long strip.

13. Attach the zipper foot. With raw edges even, sew a piping strip to the right side of the shirring strip along each of the long edges (Figure 4).

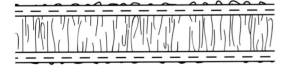

Figure 4
Sew piping to both long
edges of shirred strips.

14. Fold each pillow circle in half and then in half again and clip the folds at the raw edges to quarter-mark the circle (Figure 5).

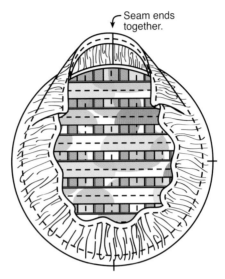

Figure 5
Match centers and sew
boxing strip to pillow front.

15. With right sides facing and the boxing strip on top, match the center snip on the boxing strip to a snip on a top pillow circle. Pin the boxing strip to the circle perimeter and when the two ends meet, mark the seam line on both sides. The seam allowance will be about ½–¾ inch wide. Undo enough pins to stitch the joining seam and press it open. Re-pin the edge to the circle and then stitch in place (Figure 5).

16. Pin and stitch the remaining edge of the boxing strip to the remaining circle for the pillow back. Leave a 12-inch-long opening for turning.

17. Turn the pillow cover right side out through the opening. Turn under the opening edge on the pillow back and slipstitch in place along the piping stitching line.

Tutti Frutti Roll

Materials for Tutti Frutti Roll

- ⅞ yard 54-inch-wide drapery sheer with burnout design (or ¾ yard 44/45-inch-wide burnout fashion-fabric sheer) for the center panel and pillow ends
- 1 yard 44/45-inch-wide lightweight linen or silk for the pillow cover
- 1 yard 45-60-inch-wide lightweight fusible knit or weft-insertion interfacing
- 2 yards narrow fringe trim in coordinating color for center panel
- 1 yard strong cord or narrow braid for the drawstring closure at each end
- 6 x 32-square piece of Sew Like Knitting sewing grid with 1¼-inch squares
  OR
- 8 x 32-inch strip of tear-away stabilizer and fine-tip permanent marking pen
- Temporary spray adhesive
- All-purpose thread to match the fabrics
- Rotary cutter, mat and ruler
- Optional: Open-toe embroidery foot
- Optional: Needle-nose tweezers
- Basic sewing tools and equipment

Cutting for Tutti Fruitti Roll

- From the length of the linen (not across the fabric width), cut three 6½ x 29-inch strips for the pillow cover and two 5 x 29-inch strips for the pillow ends. Cut the same strips from the fusible interfacing and apply the interfacing to the wrong side of each piece following the manufacturer's directions.
- From the remaining linen or scrap cotton, cut two 2 x 29-inch strips for the drawstring casings at the pillow ends.
- From one end of the sheer fabric, cut two 5 x 29-inch panels along the lengthwise grain (parallel to the selvages) for the pillow ends.
- Fold the remaining selvage end of the fabric on a true 45-degree angle with the selvage edge along the crosswise straight of grain. Cut enough ¾-inch-wide strips to equal 200 inches.

Assembly for Tutti Frutti Roll

Project Note: *Use ½-inch-wide seam allowances unless otherwise directed.*

1. Place each 5 x 29-inch sheer panel face up on top of the right side of a corresponding linen or silk panel. Pin in place or use a light coat of temporary spray adhesive to adhere the layers. Machine baste a scant ½ inch from both long edges.

2. If you are making your own sewing grid with stabilizer, draw a 5 x 32 square grid of 1¼-inch squares on the stabilizer. Otherwise, use the 6 x 32-square piece of Sew Like Knitting sewing grid.

3. If the bias strips are not already stacked in pairs, do so now. It doesn't matter if they are not the same length. Place on a tray close to the sewing machine.

4. Choose the three longest sets of strip pairs from the tray. Center one pair over the center line on the sewing grid and stitch in place along the grid line. If your strips are not long enough, simply choose another single or set as needed and tuck the short end under the end already on the grid. Lap by at least ½ inch and continue stitching until you reach the end of the grid. Sew the remaining long pairs to the grid lines to the right and left of the first row of strips (Figure 6).

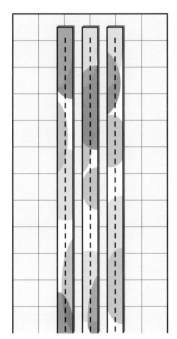

Figure 6
Sew layered strips to 3 vertical
lines on sewing grid.

5. Add strip pairs to all short grid lines in the same manner. Turn the grid over and grasp both long edges. Tug the tissue lightly to help break it away from the stitching; continue down the length of the strip. Remove the tissue, using the tweezers as needed to remove stubborn bits that may be trapped under the stitches.

6. Apply a light coat of temporary spray adhesive to the right side of one 6½ x 29-inch linen or silk strip. Center the strip right side up (short

grid strips on top) on top of the linen and smooth into place, keeping the lengthwise and crosswise strips as straight and true to the grainline as possible. Trim the strip to 5 inches wide, taking care to keep the center strip centered in the panel. Trim the panel to 29 inches long.

7. Sew a length of contrast trim to each long edge of the panel.

8. Arrange the pillow pieces as shown in Figure 7 and sew together with ½-inch-wide seams. Press the outermost seams toward the outer edges and then topstitch ¼ inch from the seamline through all layers.

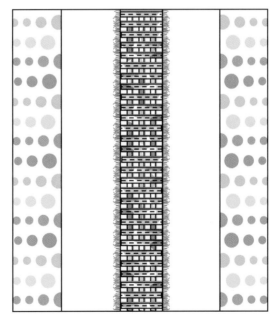

Figure 7
Pillow Cover Assembly

9. Fold the panel in half lengthwise and pin with raw edges even and seamlines matching. Stitch. Turn right side out.

10. With raw edges even and wrong sides facing, fold each 1¾-inch-wide strip in half lengthwise and press. Turn under and press ¼ inch one short end of each 1¾ x 30-inch strip.

11. Fold the strip in half lengthwise with wrong sides facing and press. Beginning at the seamline, pin and stitch a strip to each short end of the pillow cover. Turn under the end even with the first and trim excess before completing the seam (Figure 8)

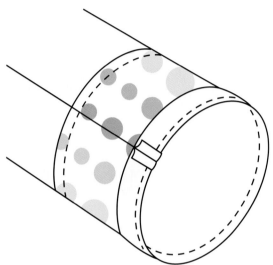

Figure 8
Sew folded strip to pillow cover at each end; turn ends at seam line.

12. Turn the strip to the inside and press. Stitch ½ inch from the edge of the fabric tube to create the drawstring casing with an opening

at the seamline. Cut the cord into two equal lengths and thread each one through a casing. (Figure 9).

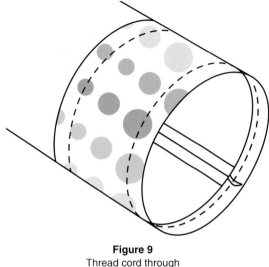

Figure 9
Thread cord through casing opening.

13. Insert the pillow into the tube and center it. Draw up the fullness to fit and tie in a secure over-hand knot. Tuck the cord ends inside the pillow.

14. Optional: Cover the gathered ends with a large covered button, or tuck a circle of the linen inside the opening and use fabric adhesive to adhere it to the end of the pillow form. ◆

In the Boudoir

Pillows are a natural choice for decorative accents in the bedroom. Luxurious fabrics, simple cottons and decorator fabrics are equally at home as accessories or to complement the bed or comfortable seating in the boudoir.

Elegant in Ecru

DESIGNS BY PAM LINDQUIST

Beautiful decorator fabrics and tone-on-tone trims add up to elegant pillow accents for a romantic bedroom setting.

Finished Size
Draped Elegance: 18 x 22 inches
   (without flanges)
Beaded Diamonds: 12 x 18 x 2 inches
Fringed Pouf: 12 inches in diameter

Draped Elegance

Materials for Draped Elegance
• 54/60-inch-wide decorator fabrics
   ⁷/₈ yard ecru brocade for pillow front and back
   ⁵/₈ yard ecru taffeta for pillow flange
• 20 x 24-inch piece lightweight quilt batting
• 20 x 24-inch piece muslin
• 2½ yards ²²/₃₂-inch-diameter cotton cord
• 20-inch-long all-purpose zipper
• 18 x 22-inch knife-edge pillow form
• All-purpose thread to match fabrics
• Hand-sewing needle and buttonhole thread
• Rotary cutter, mat and ruler
• Zipper foot
• Basic sewing tools and equipment

Cutting for Draped Elegance
• From the brocade fabric, cut one 19 x 23-inch rectangle for the pillow front. Cut one 14 x 23-inch rectangle and one 8 x 23-inch rectangle for the pillow back with zippered closure.
• From the taffeta fabric, cut two 6 x 24½-inch strips for the side flanges, two 6 x 28½-inch strips for the top and bottom flanges and four 6 x 14-inch rectangles for the corner knots.
• From the ²²/₃₂-inch-diameter cotton cord, cut two pieces 18 inches long and two pieces 22 inches long.

Assembly for Draped Elegance

Project Note: *Use ½-inch-wide seam allowances unless otherwise directed.*

1. Position the 20 x 24-inch piece of batting on top of the 20 x 24-inch piece of muslin. Center the 19 x 23-inch brocade rectangle on top and baste the layers together. Trim the excess batting and backing even with the brocade rectangle.

2. Mark the centers at each short end of the 6-inch-wide flange strips. Using rotary-cutting tools, cut a 45-degree angle on each side of the mark at each end to create points (Figure 1).

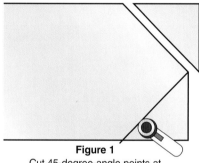

Figure 1
Cut 45-degree-angle points at
each end of 6" flange strips.

3. With right sides facing and raw edges even, sew each long flange to a short flange. End the stitching ½ inch from the raw edge as shown in Figure 2. Sew the flange pairs together in the same manner. Finger-press the seam allowances open or use only the tip of the iron to press the seams open.

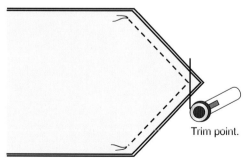

Figure 2
Sew along long flange to a short one,
ending stitching ¹/₂" from long edges.

4. Turn the flange right side out. Position a 22-inch-long piece of cotton cord into the top and bottom flanges next to the fold. Position the 18-inch-long pieces in the side flanges. Align the raw edges of each part of the flange and pin. Machine-baste a scant ½ inch from the raw edges all around the flange (Figure 3).

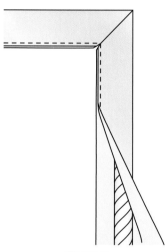

Figure 3
Insert cotton cord inside flange
sections: Baste raw edges together.

5. With raw edges even, pin one edge of the flange to the right side of the pillow front. Machine-baste in place (Figure 4). Repeat to add the remaining flange edges to the pillow top. The openings left in the diagonal seams will allow you turn the corners easily.

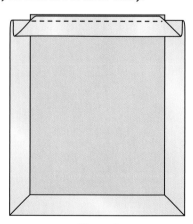

Figure 4
Sew flange to each edge of pillow top.

6. With right sides together, fold each 6 x 14-inch rectangle in half lengthwise. Stitch ½ inch from the three raw edges, leaving a 2-inch-long opening in the center of the long edge for turning. Trim the seam allowances to ¼ inch and clip the corners. Turn right side out, turning the opening edges in. Slipstitch the opening closed. Tie the strip into a loose knot. Repeat for remaining bows (Figure 5).

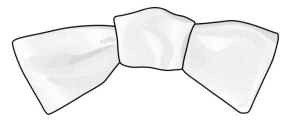

Figure 5
Tie each strip into loose knot.

7. With the 23-inch long edges aligned, sew the two back panels together using a ¾-inch-wide seam allowance. Stitch the first 1½ inches and backstitch. Change to a basting-length stitch for the next 20 inches. Backstitch. Return to the normal stitch length and complete the seam (Figure 6). Press the seam open.

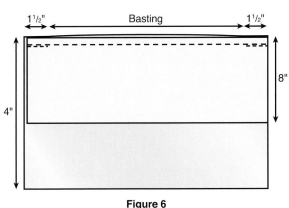

Figure 6
Sew back panels together.

8. Insert the zipper in the seam using a lapped zipper application as shown on page 15.

9. UNZIP THE ZIPPER. With right sides together and raw edges even, pin the pillow front with flange to the pillow back. Make sure the flanges are tucked completely inside the layers. Stitch ½ inch from the raw edges all around (Figure 7). Turn the pillow cover right side out through the zipper opening.

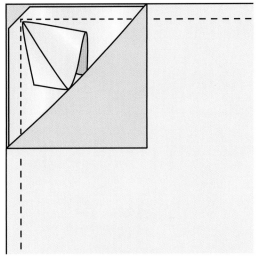

Figure 7
Sew pillow back to pillow front with flange inside.

10. Using a needle and buttonhole thread, baste from the inner to outer corner along each flange seam line. Draw up the basting to gather and secure with several neat backstitches (Figure 8).

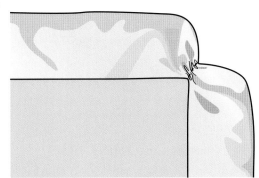

Figure 8
Gather each flange corner along seam.

11. Hand-tack a knot to each corner on the front of the pillow cover.

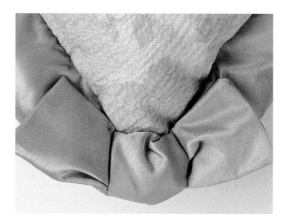

Beaded Diamonds

Materials for Beaded Diamonds
- 54-inch-wide decorator fabric
    - ½ yard heavyweight ecru taffeta for the pillow front
    - 1 yard ecru brocade fabric for the pillow back and boxing strip
- 1 yard 44/45-inch-wide muslin for the pillow insert and pillow-front backing
- 15 x 21-inch piece quilt batting
- 6 yards ¼-inch-wide grosgrain ribbon
- 4 yards ⅜-inch-diameter cord
- 16-inch-long zipper
- Polyester fiberfill
- Decorative beads of your choice or substitute small buttons
- Air-soluble marking pen or tailor's chalk
- All-purpose thread to match fabrics
- Hand-sewing needle and thread for attaching beads
- Rotary cutter with a 60-degree cutting line, mat and ruler
- Zipper foot
- Basic sewing tools and equipment

Cutting for Beaded Diamonds
- From the taffeta fabric, cut one 13 x 19-inch rectangle for the pillow front.
- From the brocade fabric, cut one 5¾ x 19-inch and one 8¾ x 19-inch rectangle for the pillow back. Also cut three 3 x 54-inch strips for the piping and two 3 x 54-inch boxing strips.
- From the muslin fabric, cut two 3 x 42-inch boxing strips and two 13 x 19-inch rectangles for the pillow insert.
- From the remaining muslin, cut one 15 x 21-inch rectangle for the pillow-front backing.

Assembly for Beaded Diamonds
Project Note: *Use ½-inch-wide seam allowances unless otherwise directed.*

1. Refer to Figure 1 for steps 1 and 2. Use an air-soluble marking pen or tailor's chalk and a rotary-cutting ruler to mark a diamond grid with diagonal lines spaced 3 inches apart on the right side of the 13 x 19-inch taffeta rectangle.

2. Pin the ¼-inch-wide grosgrain ribbon along the length of one line. Cut the ribbon ends even with the edges of the pillow top. Edgestitch the ribbon in place. Continue pinning and stitching the ribbon to the remaining lines on the pillow top. Work across the pillow top in one direction and then in the opposite direction.

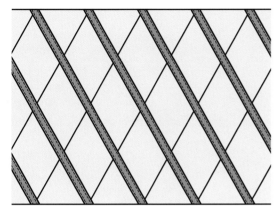

Figure 1
Sew grosgrain ribbon to diamond grid
in one direction and then the other.

3. Using needle and thread, attach decorative beads in the center of the ribboned diamonds.

4. Place the 15 x 21-inch piece of batting on top of the 15 x 21-inch piece of muslin. Center the pillow top on the batting and baste the layers together. Trim the batting and backing even with the raw edges of the pillow top.

5. Sew the short ends of the two 3 x 54-inch brocade strips to make one continuous length. Use this strip to cover the ⅜-inch-diameter cord to make the piping as shown page 12 for making fabric-covered welting. Trim the piping seam allowance to ½ inch wide.

6. Refer to Figure 2 for steps 6 and 7. Beginning at the bottom edge of the pillow front and with raw edges even, pin the piping to the pillow cover, rounding the corners as shown. Clip the piping seam allowance as needed for a smoothly rounded corner.

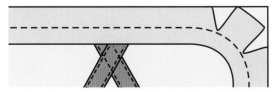

Figure 2
Sew piping to pillow top.

7. With the zipper foot attached and adjusted to the right of the needle, stitch the piping to the pillow top, overlapping the ends as shown in Figure 14 on page 13.

8. Layer the two back panels with right sides together, matching raw edges along a 19-inch-long edge. Using a ¾-inch-wide seam allowance, stitch the first 1½ inches and then backstitch. Change to a basting-length stitch and stitch the next 16 inches; backstitch. Change to the normal stitch length and complete the seam (Figure 3). Press the seam open.

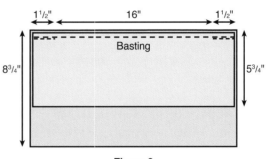

Figure 3
Sew back panels together.

9. Attach the zipper foot and insert a lapped zipper following the directions on page 15. Remove the basting.

10. Position and stitch piping to the pillow back as you did for the pillow front in steps 6 and 7.

11. Refer to Figure 4 on page 114 for steps 11 and 12. Sew the 3-inch-wide boxing strips together to make one long strip. Press the seam open. With right sides facing and raw edges even, center the seam of the boxing strip along one long edge of the pillow front and pin; pin the strip to the pillow front around all edges, meeting at the center on the remaining long edge; trim the excess boxing strip, leaving a ½-inch-wide seam allowance. Unpin as needed to sew the ends together and press the seam open. Re-pin the boxing strip in place and stitch ½ inch from the raw edges all around.

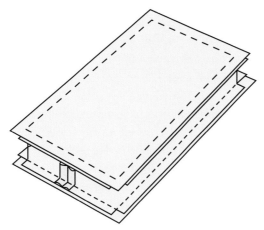

Figure 4
Sew front and back to boxing strip.

12. *Unzip the zipper* in the pillow back. Pin and stitch the remaining raw edge of the boxing strip to the pillow back. Turn the pillow cover right side out.

13. Sew the two 3 x 42-inch muslin strips together to make one long boxing strip for the pillow insert. Sew the boxing strip to one of the 13 x 19-inch muslin rectangles as you did for the pillow cover. Sew the remaining rectangle to the boxing strip, leaving a 6-inch-long opening in one long seam for turning.

14. Turn the muslin pillow cover right side out; stuff with polyester fiberfill to the desired firmness. Slipstitch or machine-stitch the opening edges together as shown on page 19.

15. Insert the pillow form into the pillow cover and zip the zipper.

Fringed Pouf

Materials for Fringed Pouf
- ¾ yard 54-inch-wide ecru taffeta decorator fabric for the pillow cover
- 13-inch-diameter circle lightweight quilt batting
- ½ yard 44/45-inch-wide muslin
- 2 yards 1½-inch-wide decorative fringe (or make your own as directed on page 116)
- 12-inch-diameter knife-edge pillow insert (polyester fiberfill)
- All-purpose thread to match fabrics
- Hand-sewing needle
- Rotary cutter, mat and ruler
- Basic sewing tools and equipment

Cutting for Fringed Pouf
- From the ecru taffeta fabric, cut one 7 x 54-inch strip for the gathered pillow top.
- From the remaining taffeta fabric, cut one 13-inch-diameter circle for the pillow back.
- From the muslin, cut two 13-inch-diameter circles for the pillow front and back underlining.

Assembly for Fringed Pouf

Project Note: *Use ½-inch-wide seam allowances unless otherwise directed.*

1. Using a ¼-inch-wide seam, sew the short ends of the 7 x 54-inch taffeta strip together with right sides facing to make a circle. Press the seam open.

2. Machine-baste a scant ½ inch and again ¼ inch from each long edge of the circle. Leave long thread tails (Figure 1).

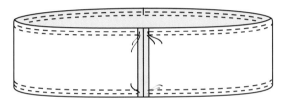

Figure 1
Machine-baste ¼" and ½"
from both edges

3. Quarter-mark both raw edges, using the seam as one of the marks. Quarter-mark the outer edge of the 13-inch muslin circle by folding it in half and then in half again and making a mark at each fold.

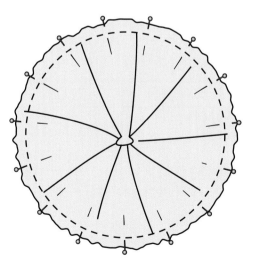

Figure 2
Draw up gathers.
Pin to muslin circle. Stitch.

4. Refer to Figure 2 for steps 4 and 5. Matching quarter marks, pin one edge of the circle strip to one edge of the 13-inch muslin circle. Draw up the bobbin threads to gather the strip to fit the outer edge of the circle. Adjust the gathers evenly and pin in place. Machine-baste a scant ½ inch from the raw edge.

5. Pull the bobbin threads on the remaining side edge to create the gathered center. Tie off the gathering threads securely.

6. With right sides together, pin the heading of the decorator fringe along the outer edge of the pillow top and join the ends neatly. Baste in place.

7. To make the center pompom, roll the remaining fringe (jelly-roll fashion), keeping the header edges even. Baste the fringe end to the rolled fringe to secure (Figure 3).

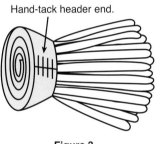

Hand-tack header end.

Figure 3
Roll fringe into pompom.

8. Place the rolled fringe pompom over the gathered seam allowances in the center of the pillow top. Hand-sew securely in place.

9. Place the 13-inch-diameter batting circle on top of the 13-inch muslin circle. With the right side up, smooth the 13-inch taffeta circle for the pillow back in place on top of the batting. Baste the layers together a scant ½ inch from the raw edges.

10. With right sides together, pin the pillow back to the pillow top. Stitch the layers together, leaving an 8-inch-long opening for turning. Turn the pillow cover right side out through the opening and insert the pillow form. Slipstitch the opening closed. ◆

Make Your Own Designer Fringe

Materials

- 1 skein textured designer yarn for the fringe
- 1 x 60-inch piece soft ribbon or bias-cut strip of fabric in color to match yarn
- 2 (5 x 30-inch) strips Perfect Pattern Paper or 2 (5 x 30-inch) strips tissue paper
- Cellophane tape
- Double-stick basting tape
- Sewing machine

1. If you are using tissue paper strips, draw a grid of 1-inch squares on each one. Tape the two 5-inch-wide strips of Perfect Pattern Paper or tissue paper together, end to end to make a 60-inch-long strip.

2. Remove the protective paper on one side of the basting tape and center it in the center of the gridded strip. Remove the remaining protective paper. Center the 1-inch-wide ribbon or fabric strip over the exposed basting tape and finger-press into place (Figure 1).

3. Using the grid as a guide, arrange the yarn in a back and forth pattern of loops between the second and fourth grid lines on the paper. Pin in place along the center as you work. Stitch the yarn in place through the center of the center square in the grid to secure it to the ribbon or fabric strip (Figure 2).

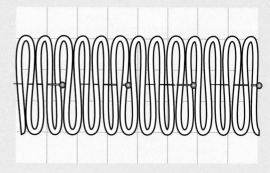

Figure 2
Loop and pin yarn to ribbon. Stitch through center, removing pins as you reach them.

4. Remove the tissue paper and the basting tape.

5. Fold the fringe in half with loops even and the raw edges of the ribbon or fabric strip aligned. Stitch ¼ inch from the raw edges (Figure 3).

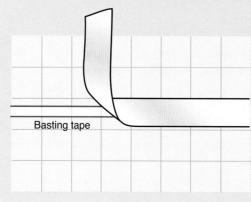

Figure 1
Finger-press ribbon onto exposed basting tape.

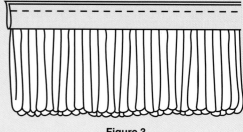

Figure 3
Sew ribbon edges together.

Boudoir Beauties

DESIGNS BY CAROL ZENTGRAF

Create these luscious pillows for bedroom accents in assorted shapes and sizes using elegant tone-on-tone fabrics accented with beautiful trims. To design panels and borders for any shape or size pillow, simply draw the desired shapes on pattern tracing cloth or paper and add ½-inch-wide seam allowances to each cut edge.

Finished Sizes
Boudoir Elegance: 18 inches square
Elegance on a Roll: 6 inches in diameter x 27
   inches long, including the fabric extensions

Boudoir Elegance

Materials for Boudoir Elegance
- Coordinating 54-inch-wide tone-on-tone
   decorator fabrics
   13-inch square floral brocade for pillow-top
      center
   ⅝ yard geometric brocade for borders and
      pillow back
- 1¾ yards each of two coordinating 1- and
   1½-inch-wide flat trims
- 2¼ yards coordinating tassel fringe with
   decorative header
- 18-inch-square pillow form

- Air-soluble marking pen or dressmaker's chalk
- Ruler or straightedge
- Permanent fabric adhesive
- Self-adhesive, double-sided basting tape
- All-purpose thread to match fabrics and trims
- Optional: Polyester fiberfill
- Rotary cutter, mat and ruler
- Basic sewing tools and equipment

Assembly for Boudoir Elegance

Project Note: *Use ½-inch-wide seam allowances throughout.*

1. From the geometric brocade, cut one 19-inch square for the pillow back and four 4 x 19-inch border strips.

2. Fold the center square for the pillow top in quarters and snip the folds to mark the centers. Fold each border strip in half and snip the fold to mark the center.

3. With right sides facing and center snips matching, sew a border strip to one edge of the center square. Begin and end the seam precisely ½ inch from the raw edge at each corner. Excess border should extend at each end of the seam (Figure 1). Press the seam toward the border strip.

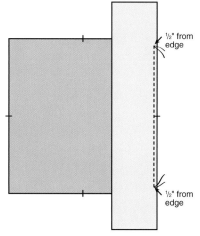

Figure 1
Sew border strip to square;
begin and end ¹/₂" from edge of square.

4. Repeat step 3 to add the remaining border strips to the square.

5. To miter each corner, fold the corner in half diagonally with right sides together and the two adjacent border strips even. Turn the pressed seam allowance down temporarily and pin the border strips together. Use a ruler or

straightedge and the marking pen to draw a line from the end of the stitching to the outer corner of the layered borders as shown in Figure 2.

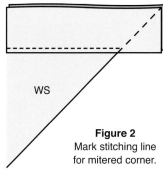

Figure 2
Mark stitching line
for mitered corner.

6. Stitch along the line and then trim the excess fabric, leaving a ¼-inch-wide seam allowance. Press the seam allowance open (Figure 3).

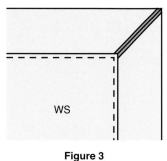

Figure 3
Stitch and trim corner
seams; press open.

7. Lap one edge of the 1½-inch-wide flat trim over one long edge of the 1-inch-wide trim and edgestitch together.

8. Apply basting tape along both long edges on the wrong side of the assembled trim. Remove the backing paper from only what will be the inner edge of the trim on the pillow cover.

9. Refer to Figure 4 on page 120. Beginning with 2 inches of trim extending from one corner of the seam on the pillow top, position the trim over the seam line. Make mitered folds at each corner as you work. Keep the trim straight and evenly spaced from the outer edge of the pillow square. Remove the backing from the remaining basting tape at the outer edge of the trim and adhere to the pillow top. To finish the last corner, turn under the trim end to create a

mitered fold; secure with pins or a small piece of basting tape. Trim the excess trim at both ends. Stitch the trim to the panel along both edges and along the edge of each mitered corner fold.

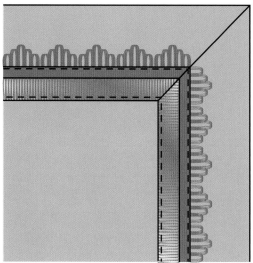

Figure 4
Stitch trim to pillow top.

10. With right sides together, sew the pillow front and back together, leaving a 10-inch-long opening in one edge for turning.

Note: If you prefer a pillow cover that you can remove for cleaning, insert an invisible zipper in one seam before sewing the front and back together. See Invisible Zipper Installation on page 16. **Unzip the zipper** *before sewing the front and back together.*

11. Trim the corners and turn the cover right side out. Turn under and press ½ inch at the opening edges.

12. Insert the pillow form and add bits of polyester fiberfill to the corners if needed to fill them out (see page 20). Slipstitch the opening edges together.

13. Use fabric adhesive to glue the header of the tassel trim in place around the outer edge of the front panel. Make a mitered fold at each corner as you reach it.

Elegance on a Roll

Materials for Elegance on a Roll
- Coordinating 54-inch-wide tone-on-tone decorator fabrics
    ⅓ yard floral brocade for center panel
    ¼ yard geometric brocade for inner borders
    ½ yard solid for outer borders and ends
- 1¼ yards tassel fringe with decorative header
- 2½ yards ⅞-inch-wide decorative flat trim
- 6 x 20-inch neckroll pillow form
- 2 rubber bands
- Self-adhesive, double-sided basting tape
- Permanent fabric adhesive
- All-purpose thread to match fabrics and trims
- Rotary cutter, mat and ruler
- Basic sewing tools and equipment

Cutting for Elegance on a Roll
- Cut the following pieces from the fabric you've selected for each section: one 9 x 20-inch center panel, two 4 x 20-inch strips for the inner borders and two 14 x 20-inch strips for the outer borders.
- From the flat trim, cut four 20-inch lengths and two 5-inch lengths.
- Cut the tassel trim into two 20-inch lengths.

Assembly for Elegance on a Roll

Project Note: *Use ½-inch-wide seam allowances throughout.*

1. Sew the 4 x 20-inch inner border strips to the long edges of the center panel. Press the seams open. Add the outer border strips to each side and press the seams open (Figure 1).

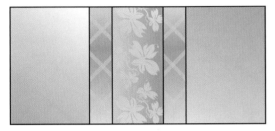

Figure 1
Sew pillow panels together.

2. Refer to Figure 2 for steps 2–4. Position the header of the fringe trim along the outer border seam line on each end of the panel and stitch in place along the upper and lower edges of the header.

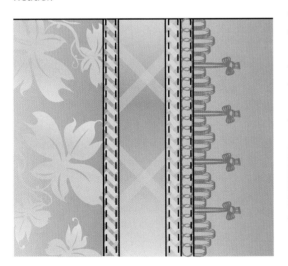

Figure 2
Position and stitch
trims in place.

3. Apply basting tape on the wrong side in the center of each 20-inch length of flat trim. Remove the paper on two of the pieces. Position each piece with one edge over the header edge of the fringe trim. Stitch in place along both long edges.

4. Remove the protective paper on the remaining pieces and center each one over the inner-border seam lines. Stitch in place along both long edges of each piece.

5. Fold the pieced pillow panel in half with short raw edges even and the seam lines aligned. Pin and stitch. Press the seam open and turn the tube right side out.

6. At each raw edge of the tube, turn under and press ½ inch. Turn under an additional 4 inches at each end and press. Stitch close to the inner edge.

7. Insert and center the pillow form inside the cover. Gather each end of the cover at the end of the pillow form and secure with a rubber band, wrapped tight. Evenly arrange the gathers that form. Use fabric adhesive to glue a 5-inch flat trim length around the gathers of each end, covering the rubber band. Turn under and glue the trim ends to finish. ◆

Embroidered Beauties

Embellishment is the beauty secret of many designer pillows. In addition to trims, machine embroidery is a wonderful way to accent a border strip. In keeping with a tone-on-tone color scheme, use a thread color that's one or two shades darker than the border strip. Cut and embroider the border strips individually; then sew them to the center panel as instructed on page 118.

Floral Romance

DESIGN BY BARBARA WEILAND

Capture silk flowers from the craft department to float on a silken ground for this romantic boudoir pillow. Bound edges create a narrow flange around the outer edge. Transform this project into a ring bearer's pillow by eliminating the center flower and adding ribbons or a pocket to the center square for the rings.

Finished Size

16¾ inches square

Materials

- ¾ yard pink silk dupioni for pillow front, back and binding
- 18 x 36-inch piece lightweight fusible weft-insertion, woven or knit interfacing
- 12 yards ⅛- or ³⁄₁₆-inch-wide ribbon for pillow top and ribbon tassels
- 9 silk flowers, 2½–3-inch diameter
- ¼-inch-wide strips of paper-backed fusible web
- 13 small pearls or coordinating beads
- 17 (2-hole) flat pink buttons, ⅜- or ½-inch diameter
- 14-inch-long invisible zipper (shorten a longer one if necessary)
- Air-soluble or chalk marker
- All-purpose thread to match fabric
- 16-inch-square pillow form
- Rotary cutter, mat and ruler
- Basic sewing tools and equipment

Cutting

- From the pink silk, cut two 2½ x 42-inch straight-grain strips for the outer-edge binding.
- From the remaining silk, cut the pieces shown in Figure 1 on page 124.
- From the fusible interfacing, cut the same pieces shown in Figure 1.

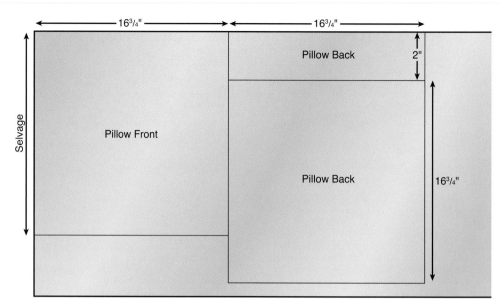

Figure 1
Cut silk pieces for pillow.

Assembly

1. Following the manufacturer's directions, apply the fusible interfacing to the wrong side of each corresponding piece of silk.

2. Following the directions on page 16, insert the invisible zipper between the two back pieces. Be sure to center the zipper along the length of the seam so there is unstitched seam allowance beyond both the upper and lower stop (Figure 2). Complete the seam beyond the lower and upper ends of the zipper as directed on page 17.

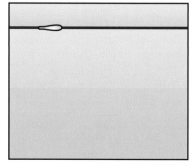

Figure 2
Center invisible zipper
in back seam.

3. On the right side of the pillow front, draw ribbon placement lines as shown in Figure 3. Also mark the center of each of the squares in the grid you have drawn.

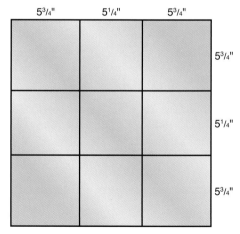

Figure 3
Mark ribbon placement.

4. Position and pin ribbon over the grid lines in one direction and stitch in place. Use a straight stitch through the center or a narrow zigzag stitch. Position, pin and stitch ribbons in the opposite direction.

5. One at a time, separate the flower petals from the stem and reassemble each one at the center of a square on the pillow top. Pin in place.

6. Hand- or machine-tack each flower in place. (On the machine, adjust for a narrow bartack stitch and drop the feed dogs.) Hand-sew a flat button in place over the tacking stitch with one or two stitches, and then add a pearl or bead and sew in place securely, going through the button several more times. Secure with a few backstitches on the underside of the pillow top.

7. With raw edges even and wrong sides facing, pin the pillow front and back together. Machine-baste a scant ⅜ inch from the raw edges.

8. Using bias seams as shown on page 11, sew the two 2½ x 42-inch strips together to create one long strip. Press the seam open, and then fold the strip in half lengthwise with raw edges even and wrong sides together. Press. Unfold at one end and turn under at a 45-degree angle; press and trim the excess, leaving a ¼-inch turn-under allowance. Refold (Figure 4).

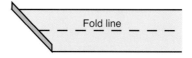

Figure 4
Turn end at 45-degree
angle; press.

9. Beginning in the center of one side, pin the binding to the pillow cover with raw edges even. Begin stitching 1 inch below the folded end and use a ⅜-inch-wide seam allowance. End the stitching precisely ⅜ inch from the first corner. Backstitch, clip the threads and remove the work from the machine. Rotate the pillow cover counterclockwise (Figure 5).

Figure 5
End stitching ⅜"
from raw edge at corner.

10. Fold the binding as shown to make a mitered turn (Figure 6). Pin and stitch, ending ⅜ inch from the next corner.

a

b

Figure 6
Fold bias to miter the corner.

11. Continue in this manner to bind the remaining edges and miter the remaining corners. When you reach the starting point, trim

the excess binding, leaving enough to tuck into the open end. Pin and stitch to complete the seam (Figure 7).

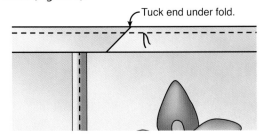

Tuck end under fold.

Figure 7
Complete the binding stitching.

12. Wrap the binding to the back of the pillow cover, making mitered folds at the corners. Slipstitch in place around the pillow and press as needed.

13. Divide the remaining ribbon into four equal lengths—about 2 yards each. Wrap each ribbon around your fingers (or a piece of cardboard 3½ inches wide). Slip the loops off your fingers and pinch together at one end, so you can stitch across the stack of ribbon loops (Figure 8).

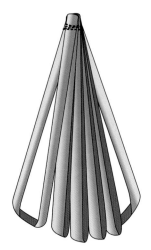

Figure 8
Stitch across ribbon loops at one end.

of each corner of the pillow. Sew a button in place on the front and back of the tassel to hide the end. After taking a few stitches through all layers and both buttons, add a pearl on the top as you did for the flowers and take several more stitches before securing the last stitches under the button on the back of the pillow top.

15. Unzip the pillow cover and tuck the pillow inside, coaxing the pillow into the corners. Add bits of polyester fiberfill in each corner to fill them out if necessary (see page 20).

16. If the flowers "pop" off the surface of the pillow too much, cut small bits of ¼-inch-wide fusible web. Tuck them under the petals toward the flower center and use the tip of the iron to fuse them in place. ◆

14. Fold the loops along the stitching and stitch through all layers to make a looped tassel. Hand- or machine-tack a tassel to the mitered area

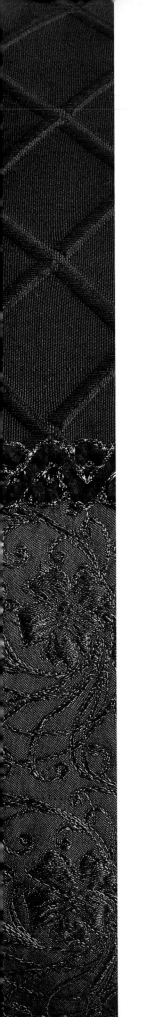

Elegantly Patched

DESIGN BY JUDY MURRAH

Accent richly colored and textured decorator fabrics with pretty trims and a nosegay to create this lovely pillow for your boudoir or a romantic living room.

Finished Size

13 x 27 inches, excluding fringe

Materials

- Decorator fabrics or remnants
    - 2 (7 x 10-inch) rectangles red Fabric #1 for pillow top
    - 2 (7 x 10-inch) rectangles red Fabric #2 for pillow top
    - 1/8 yard off-white textured solid for ruching strips
    - 1/8 yard red silk or taffeta for outer borders
    - 1/2 yard red fabric for pillow back
- 1 yard 1/2–3/4-inch-wide decorative trim for pillow-top center
- 1 yard wide braid tasseled trim
- 1 yard narrow red trim
- 1 yard 2-inch-wide fringe trim
- 13½ x 27½-inch piece lightweight batting
- All-purpose thread to match fabrics and trims
- Silk flower nosegay for pillow center
- 1/2 yard 1-inch-wide ribbon for nosegay
- 2 (13½ x 26-inch) muslin rectangles for the pillow insert
- Polyester fiberfill for stuffing
- Rotary cutter, mat and ruler
- Basic sewing tools and equipment

Cutting

- From the off-white fabric for the ruching strips, cut two 2½ x 20-inch strips.
- From the red silk or taffeta for the outer borders, cut two 2½ x 13½-inch strips.
- From the red print for the pillow back, cut two 13½ x 16½-inch rectangles.

Assembly

Project Note: *Use ¼-inch-wide seam allowances throughout.*

1. Sew the short ends of each Fabric #1 rectangle to a Fabric #2 rectangle. Press the seams open. Sew the two units together and press the seam open (Figure 1).

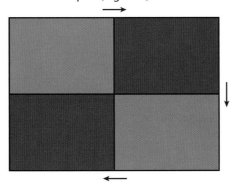

Figure 1
Sew center patches together and
press seams as directed by arrows.

2. Mark the centers on both edges of each off-white ruching strip and one edge of each outer border strip.

3. Machine-baste ⅜ inch and a scant ¼ inch from both long edges of each strip. Match the center of the ruching strip to the center of a border strip and pin in place. Draw up the bobbin threads on each side of each ruching strip. Adjust the gathers evenly and pin to the outer border with raw edges even. Machine-stitch in place. Match the center on the remaining edge of the ruching strip to the center seam in the patchwork. Adjust the gathers evenly, pin in place and stitch. Remove any basting that shows beyond the seam line. Press the seams away from the ruching strips (Figure 2).

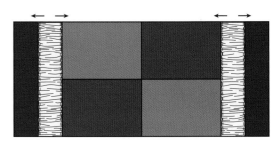

Figure 2
Sew ruching and border
units to patchwork center.

4. Smooth the pillow top in place on top of the batting rectangle. Center the ½–¾-inch decorative trim over the seam lines and pin in place. Edgestitch through all layers.

5. Apply the braid tasseled trim along the inner ruching seam lines and the narrow red trim along the outer ruching seam lines; stitch in place.

6. Cut two 14-inch pieces of fringe trim. Position the fringe header in the seam allowance at each end of the pillow top and turn under ¼ inch of the header at each end. Stitch to the pillow top along the inner edge of the header (Figure 3).

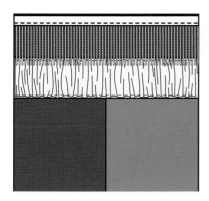

Figure 3
Sew fringe header to seam
allowance at each end of pillow top.

7. At one short end of each piece for the pillow back, turn under and press ½ inch. Turn under and press an additional inch; edgestitch in place.

8. Lap the short finished ends of the two rectangles, right side up, and adjust so the resulting rectangle is the same length (27½ inches) as the pillow top. Machine-baste ¼ inch from the raw edges in the overlap area (Figure 4).

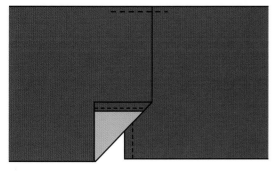

Figure 4
Overlap finished edges of back panels; baste.

9. Pin the pillow top and back together with right sides facing and raw edges even. Stitch ¼ inch from all edges. Serge or zigzag the seam allowances together for added seam strength. Turn the pillow cover right side out through the opening in the center back.

10. Sew the muslin rectangles together, leaving an 8-inch opening for turning. Turn right side out and stuff to the desired firmness. Sew the opening closed and insert in the pillow cover.

11. Wrap the 1-inch-wide ribbon around the base of the nosegay and tie in a bow. Cut ends at an angle and tack the bow to the nosegay. Hand-sew the nosegay to the pillow-top center. ◆

Provence Country Chic

DESIGNS BY CAROL ZENTGRAF

Provençal prints in bright colors and interesting shapes team up in this bevy of beautiful pillows. They're the perfect accent for a bedroom steeped in the ever-popular French country look.

Finished Sizes

Letter From Provence: 14 inches square
I Left My Heart in Provence: 14-inch heart,
   3 inches thick
Bandbox Fresh: 16 x 20 inches, excluding
   the ruffle
Provence Scallops: 25 inches square, including
   scalloped flange

Letter From Provence

Materials for Letter From Provence
• 44/45-inch-wide or wider cotton fabric
   ⅝ yard print for pillow
   ¼ yard each 2 coordinating prints for flap
• 1⅛ yards (¾-inch-wide) gimp trim
• 1 yard tassel trim with decorative header
• ¼ yard lightweight fusible interfacing
• 14-inch-square pillow form
• Rotary cutter, mat and ruler

• Air-soluble marking pen
• Pattern tracing cloth or tissue paper
• Pencil
• Permanent fabric adhesive
• All-purpose thread to match fabrics
• Basic sewing tools and equipment

Cutting for Letter From Provence

- Draw a 15-inch square on pattern tracing cloth or tissue paper. Use the ruler and a pencil to draw diagonal lines from corner to corner. Add ½-inch-wide seam allowances to the diagonal edges of one triangle and cut out for the flap pattern (Figure 1).

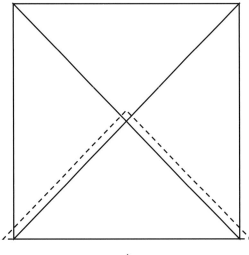

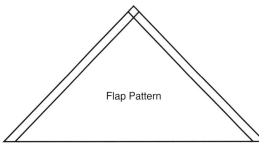

Flap Pattern

Figure 1
Draw diagonal lines through a 15" square.
Add ¹/₂" seam allowances to adjacent
sides of one triangle. Cut out.

- Use the flap pattern to cut one flap from each of the two coordinating fabrics and the fusible interfacing.
- From the print for the pillow front and back, cut two 15-inch squares.

Assembly for Letter From Provence

Project Note: *Use ½-inch-wide seam allowances unless otherwise directed.*

1. Following the manufacturer's directions, fuse the interfacing to the wrong side of one flap.

2. With right sides facing and raw edges even, sew the flaps together along the two adjacent edges, leaving the long edge unstitched. Trim the seams to ¼ inch and clip the corner at the point (Figure 2). Turn right side out. Press. Machine-baste ⅜ inch from the raw edges.

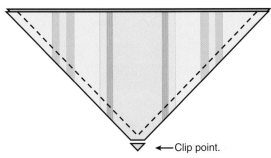

←Clip point.

Figure 2
Sew flaps together.

3. Position and stitch the tassel trim header along the finished edges on one side of the flap, mitering the trim at the point. Take care to stitch evenly, as the stitching will show on the other side of the flap. Use thread in the bobbin to match the flap fabric on the underside (Figure 3).

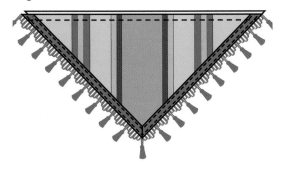

Figure 3
Sew fringe trim to flap.

4. With raw edges even, center and pin the flap to the right side of one pillow square. Pin the remaining square panel in place, sandwiching the flap between the right sides of the panels. Sew together, leaving a 10-inch-long opening in the lower edge for turning (Figure 4). Trim the corners and turn the pillow cover right side out. Turn under and press the opening edges.

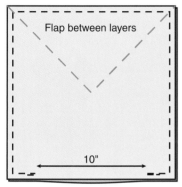

Figure 4
Sew pillow front to back.

5. Use the fabric adhesive to glue the flat gimp trim around the edges of the pillow cover. Allow to dry thoroughly.

6. Insert the pillow form and slipstitch the opening closed.

I Left My Heart in Provence

Materials for I Left My Heart in Provence
- 44/45-inch-wide or wider cotton prints
    ½ yard border print for the top and bottom panels
    ¼ yard for boxing strip
- 6 yards 1½-inch-wide grosgrain ribbon
- All-purpose thread to match fabrics
- 14 x 14 x 3-inch block Nu-Foam upholstery foam alternative
- Medium-tip permanent marker

- Sharp, heavy-duty scissors
- Pattern tracing cloth or tissue paper
- Pencil
- Liquid seam sealant
- Permanent fabric adhesive
- Ruffler attachment for sewing machine
- Basic sewing tools and equipment

Cutting for I Left My Heart in Provence
- Enlarge the heart pattern (Figure 1) onto a 16-inch square of pattern tracing paper or tissue paper. Add ½-inch-wide seam allowances all around (Figure 1).

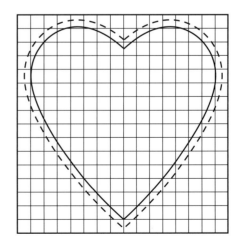

Figure 1
Draw heart shape and add
½" seam allowance all around.
1 square = 1"

• Cut out the heart pattern and use to cut two identical panels for the pillow front and back from the border-print fabric. Take care to center one border stripe in the center of the heart shape (Figure 2).

Figure 2
Cut two identical hearts
from border print.

• **Trim the seam allowance from the heart pattern piece.** Center the pattern on the foam and trace around the edges using the permanent marker. Use heavy-duty scissors to cut the heart from the foam, cutting the foam in layers rather than trying to cut all the way through the entire thickness at once.
• Cut two 4 x 24-inch strips from the boxing-strip fabric. Sew them together at a pair of short ends to make one long strip. Use a ¼-inch-wide seam allowance and press open.
• Cut the ribbon into two equal lengths for the pleated ruffle.

Assembly for I Left My Heart in Provence
***Project Note:** Use ½-inch-wide seam allowances.*

1. Attach the ruffler to your sewing machine and adjust to the desired pleat depth—follow the ruffler directions and test on scraps to determine the correct setting.

2. Feed each piece of ribbon through the ruffler to pleat each one to a length of 48 inches or slightly longer.

3. Beginning at the lower point of one heart-shaped panel, pin the ruffled ribbon to the right side with the ruffled edge even with the heart raw edge. Allow the ribbon ends to extend past the point to allow for a joining seam. Stitch to within 2 inches of the point on each side (Figure 3). Repeat with the remaining heart panel.

Figure 3
Pin and stitch ruffle to heart, leaving 2"
unstitched at each side of point.

4. Join the ribbon ends at the point of each heart panel with a narrow seam; treat the seam raw edges with liquid seam sealant. Allow to dry. Pin the ruffle to the point and complete the stitching.

5. With right sides together and the seam in the boxing strip positioned at the cleft of the heart, pin the boxing strip in place. There should be extra boxing strip extending past the point at each end. Mark the seam line for the join at the point on the wrong side at both ends of the boxing strip and sew on the line. Trim away the excess, leaving a ¼-inch-wide seam allowance. Press the seam open. Stitch the boxing strip in place (Figure 4).

Figure 4
Sew boxing strip to heart.

6. Sew the remaining heart panel to the remaining raw edge, leaving an 8-inch-long opening along one long edge of the heart for turning. Clip the seam at the cleft, taking care not to clip past the stitching (Figure 5). Turn the pillow cover right side out. Turn in and press the opening edges.

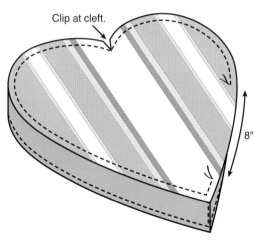

Figure 5
Sew boxing strip to remaining heart.

7. Insert the foam heart and adjust the seam lines so they sit at the edge of the heart and the ruffles extend outward. Slipstitch the opening edges together.

Bandbox Fresh

Materials for Bandbox Fresh

- 44/45-inch-wide or wider cotton fabric
  ½ yard Provençal border print for pillow front
  ¾ yard coordinating allover Provençal print for ruffles and pillow back
- 5 (1-inch-diameter) 2-hole buttons
- 16 x 20-inch knife-edge pillow insert
- All-purpose thread to match fabrics
- Ruffler attachment for sewing machine
- Rotary cutter, mat and ruler
- Basic sewing tools and equipment

Cutting for Bandbox Fresh

- From the border print fabric, cut two 9 x 17-inch panels with the selected border design along the 17-inch length. Cut one 5 x 17-inch border-design strip for the center. You may need to adjust this panel width slightly to accommodate the border-design strip of your choice, allowing for ½-inch-wide seam allowances.
- From the allover print, cut two 14 x 17-inch panels for the pillow back with envelope opening. From the remaining fabric, cut enough 4-inch-wide strips to make 8½ yards for the ruffles.

Assembly for Bandbox Fresh

Project Note: *Use ½-inch-wide seam allowances unless otherwise directed.*

1. Using bias seams (see page 11), sew the ruffle strips together to make one long piece. Press the seams open. Fold the strip in half lengthwise with wrong sides facing and press.

2. Attach the ruffler and ruffle the strip to measure about 3½–4 yards long. Test the ruffler setting first and adjust to create pleats that are about ½ inch wide on the surface with a narrow return on the underside. Refer to the directions for the ruffler.

3. Refer to Figure 1 for steps 3 and 4. With raw edges even, pin the ruffle to one long edge of the center panel for the pillow front and trim excess. Stitch ½ inch from the raw edges. Repeat with the remaining long edge of the panel.

4. With right sides together and raw edges even, sew a border panel to each long edge of the panel with the ruffle. Press the seams toward the center border panel. Evenly space and sew the buttons to the panel with 3 inches between buttons from center to center.

Press seam allowance.

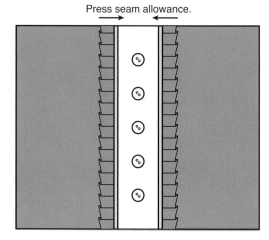

Figure 1
Assemble the pillow front.

5. Beginning at the center of the lower edge, pin the ruffle to the outer edges of the pieced front panel. Undo the ruffle stitching at each end of the ruffle strip so that you can sew the ends together. Press the seam open. Fold and re-pleat the ruffle by hand to fit the pillow edge. Clip the ruffle seam allowance at the corners as needed to make a smooth turn at each one. Stitch the ruffle to the pillow top a scant ½ inch from the raw edges (Figure 2).

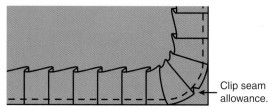

Clip seam allowance.

Figure 2
Pin and stitch ruffle to outer edge of pillow top.

6. On one long edge of each 14 x 17-inch rectangle, turn under and press 1 inch. Turn under again and press. Edgestitch along the inner pressed edge. Overlap the finished edges and adjust so the resulting panel is 17 x 21 inches. Machine-baste ⅜ inch from the raw edges in the overlapped area, creating an envelope closure (Figure 3).

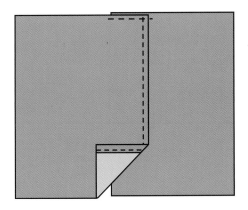

Figure 3
Lap finished edges of back panels.

7. With right sides together and raw edges even and the ruffle sandwiched between the layers, sew the pillow front and back together. Clip the corners and turn right side out. Press as needed.

8. Tuck the pillow form inside through the opening in the back of the pillow.

Provence Scallops

Materials for Provence Scallops
- 44/45-inch-wide or wider cotton
    1 yard Provençal print for pillow front and back
    1 yard muslin for the backing
- 30-inch square low-loft batting
- 12-inch-long piece ¾-inch-wide hook-and-loop tape
- All-purpose thread to match fabrics
- 22-inch-square knife-edge pillow form
- Pattern tracing cloth or tissue paper
- Chalk fabric pencil
- Rotary cutter, mat and ruler
- Yardstick
- Optional: Temporary spray adhesive
- Optional: Walking foot for the sewing machine
- Basic sewing tools and equipment

Cutting for Provence Scallops
- From the print, cut one 29-inch square for the pillow front and two 17½ x 29-inch rectangles for the pillow back with envelope closure.
- From the muslin, cut one 31-inch square.
- Trace the scallop pattern on page 142 onto pattern tracing cloth or tissue paper and cut out.

Assembly for Provence Scallops
1. Use the chalk pencil to trace around the scallop pattern at each corner and along the edges of the pillow front panel. Draw a line 3½ inches from the outer edges of the front panel for the flange stitching line. Cut the front panel along the marked scallop lines. Chalk-mark the quilting lines on the pillow front with lines ending at the flange stitching line in line with the inner points of the scallops (Figure 1 on page 140). Use a yardstick as your guide to mark the quilting lines on the front panel.

2. Smooth the batting in place on the muslin square. If desired, use temporary spray adhesive to adhere the layers. Add the pillow top, face up, and smooth into place, taking care not to disturb the marked lines. If you didn't use temporary spray adhesive, then use safety pins to hold the layers together for quilting. Note that batting and backing extend past the outer edge of the pillow front.

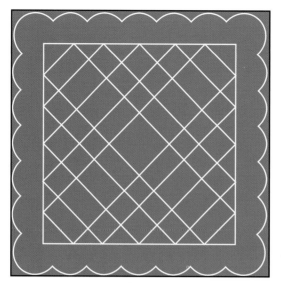

Figure 1
Draw scallops on pillow square.

3. Attach the walking foot or engage even-feed on your machine if available. Stitch on the quilting lines. Begin with the lines closest to the center and work out to the edges. Draw the thread ends through to the underside and tie off securely.

4. Machine-stitch ⅛ inch from the scalloped edges through all layers. Trim the batting and backing even with the outer scalloped edges. Machine-baste ½ inch from the scalloped edges, using a contrast color in the bobbin so it shows on the muslin side of the panel.

5. Refer to Figure 2 for steps 5 and 6. Finish one long edge of one 17½ x 29-inch rectangle with serging or turn and press a double ½-inch-wide hem. Stitch. On the remaining back panel, turn under and stitch a double ½-inch-wide hem. Center and sew the hook tape to the hemmed edge.

6. Overlap the finished edges of the panel with the hemmed edge with hook tape on top, and adjust so the resulting panel is 29 inches square.

Machine-baste ⅜ inch from the raw edges in the overlap area. Mark the position for the loop tape on the bottom panel and stitch in place.

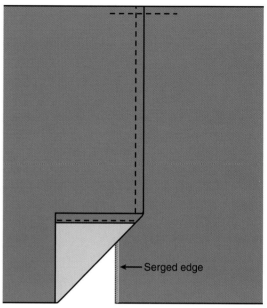

Figure 2
Prepare back panel.

7. Center the quilted front panel on the back panel with right sides facing. Stitch along the basting lines (Figure 3).

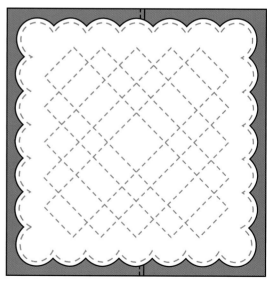

Figure 3
Stitch front panel to back panel.

8. Trim the backing panel even with the scalloped edge. Trim the seam allowance to ¼ inch and clip to but not past the stitching at the inner point of each scallop (Figure 3). Turn right side out and press.

9. Pin the front and back panels together along the flange stitching line. Stitch along the line (Figure 4).

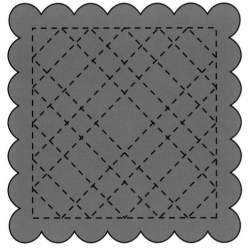

Figure 4
Stitch front to back along
stitching lines to create flange.

10. Insert the pillow form and secure the closure with the hook-and-loop tape strips. ◆

Mix-&-Match Beauties

A well-planned grouping of pillows or other fabric accessories adds a decorator touch to any room. Pulling together coordinating fabrics to mix and match can be a lot of fun when you keep the following tips in mind:

• Select at least one color to carry through in each fabric used in a grouping. This will tie them all together and give a look of continuity. For example, in the featured grouping, you'll find the same blue in each print.

• Vary the scale of the fabric prints. Two large prints used side by side can be overwhelming, while either of them will look stunning when paired with a smaller print, stripe or check.

• Use fabric design elements, such as stripes and borders, for details like ruffles or ties.

• Manufacturer's fabric collections are designed for mixing and matching. They often make the decision making easy for you by offering an array of prints in various scales, checks, stripes and coordinating solids.

Cutting Line

Stitching Line

Corner of 24-inch
square

Provence Scallops Pattern
Actual Size

Raggity Taggity

DESIGNS BY CAROL MOFFATT

No tedious clipping allowed with these rugged pillows reminiscent of raggity-edge quilts. Bias-cut strips of sturdy denim and inside-out seaming plus a toss in the wash make the pillow covers "bloom."

Finished Sizes
Make It Monotone: 24 inches square
Denim Checkerboard: 18 inches square

Make It Monotone

Materials for Make It Monotone
- 3½ yards 54/60-inch-wide light blue denim
- All-purpose thread to match fabric
- 24-inch-square knife-edge pillow form
- Rotary cutter, mat and ruler with 45-degree-angle line
- Basic sewing tools and equipment

Cutting for Make It Monotone
- Wash and press the denim.
- Fold the fabric in half lengthwise with selvages aligned, and make sure the fold is lying flat and smooth.
- Place the fabric on the cutting mat with the folded edge closest to you.
- Beginning at the lower left-hand corner of the folded fabric, position the 45-degree-angle line parallel to the fabric fold and make the first bias cut (Figure 1 on page 145).
- Continue cutting the fabric on the bias, spacing the cuts 4 inches apart across the entire piece of folded fabric. Leave the strips layered and treat each layered set as a unit during the construction. Set aside the short strips for another project. You will use only the full-length double-layer bias strips that run from selvage to fold (Figure 2 on page 145).
- Square off the angled ends of each double-layer strip (Figure 3 on page 145).

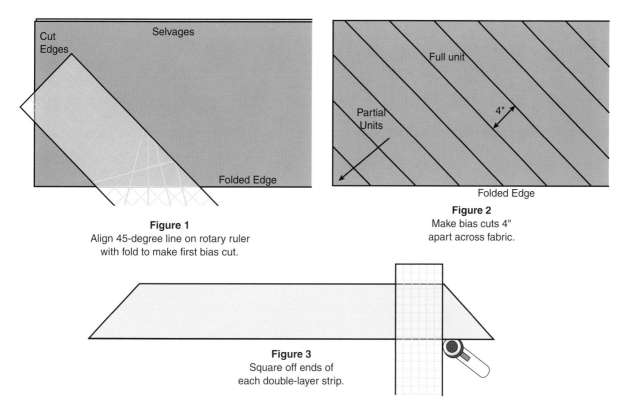

Figure 1
Align 45-degree line on rotary ruler
with fold to make first bias cut.

Figure 2
Make bias cuts 4"
apart across fabric.

Figure 3
Square off ends of
each double-layer strip.

Assembly for Make It Monotone

Project Note: *Use ½-inch-wide seam allowances throughout.*

1. Sew the double-layered strips together in pairs (Figure 4).

2. Sew four pairs together for the pillow front. Repeat for the pillow back. Place one completed unit on the cutting mat with the seam allowances on top. Cut the piece into 4-inch-wide strips. You should have eight strips. Repeat with the remaining pieced unit (Figure 5).

Figure 4
Sew double-layer strips
together in pairs (4 strips).

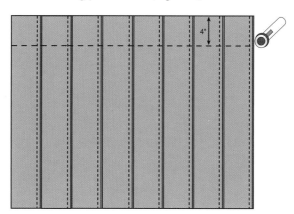

Figure 5
Sew 4 pairs together for
pillow front and pillow back.
Cut into 4"-wide units.

3. Sew eight strips together for the pillow front and repeat with the remaining strips for the pillow back. Alternate the seam-allowance direction at each intersection and pin in place before sewing (Figure 6).

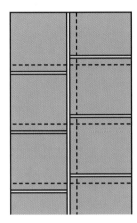

Figure 6
Sew strips together in pairs
with seam allowances in
alternate directions.

4. With the patchwork seam allowances on the outside, pin the pillow front and back together. Alternate the seam-allowance directions as you did when sewing the patchwork strips together. Machine-stitch ½ inch from three raw edges, backstitching at the beginning and end of the stitching. ***Machine-baste*** the remaining edges together.

5. Wash the pillow cover in the washing machine and dry in the dryer to make the raw-edge seam allowances "bloom."

6. Remove the basting and insert the pillow form. Pin the edges together and stitch, pushing the pillow form out of the way and using a zipper foot if necessary to complete the seam. If you prefer, you can hand-sew the last seam using a close backstitch.

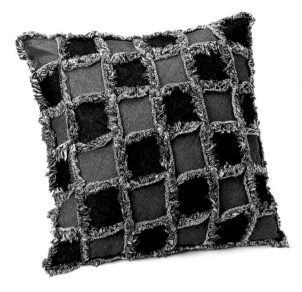

Denim Checkerboard

Materials for Denim Checkerboard

- 54/60-inch-wide 100 percent cotton denim
  1 yard light blue
  1 yard dark blue
- 18-inch-square knife-edge pillow form
- All purpose thread to match fabrics
- Rotary cutter, mat and ruler with
  45-degree-angle line
- Basic sewing tools and equipment

Cutting for Denim Checkerboard

- Prepare each piece of fabric and then fold and cut into double-layer strips as directed in Cutting for Make It Monotone (Figures 1 and 2 on page 145). You will need six light denim double-layer strips and six dark denim double-layer strips.
- Square off the ends of the strips as shown in Figure 3 on page 145.

Assembly for Denim Checkerboard

Project Note: *Use ½-inch-wide seam allowances throughout.*

1. Pin and sew a light denim double-layer bias strip to each dark denim double-layer bias strip. Sew three of these units together for the pillow front and three for the pillow back (Figure 7). Cut each panel into six 4-inch-wide strips.

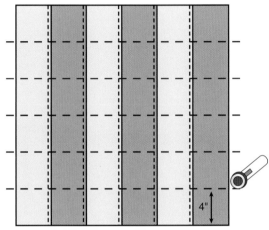

4"

Figure 7
Sew units together.
Cut into 4"-wide strips.
Make 2.

2. Arrange the strips checkerboard fashion and pin together with seam allowances alternating at each intersection as shown in Figure 6 on page 146. Stitch (Figure 8).

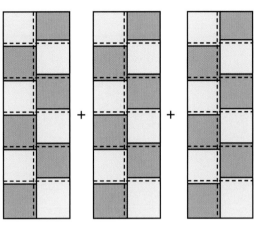

Figure 8
Sew units together
for pillow front and back.
Make 2.

3. Complete the pillow following steps 4–6 for Make It Monotone. ◆

Bow Regards

DESIGN BY MARTA ALTO

Tie up a pretty plaid in lush contrasting bows. Coordinating brushed fringe adds a colorful accent to this decidedly feminine pillow.

Finished Size
14 x 18 inches, excluding trim

Materials
• ½ yard 45-inch-wide plaid taffeta or similar fabric for the pillow front and back
• 1 yard contrasting satin or taffeta for the bows
• 2¼ yards coordinating 1½-inch-wide brushed fringe trim
• 14 x 18-inch knife-edge pillow form
• All-purpose thread to match fabrics
• Rotary cutter, mat and ruler
• Basic sewing tools and equipment

Cutting
• From the plaid, cut two identical 14½ x 18½-inch panels for the pillow front and back. Cut the first one from the plaid, centering the design in the panel; use the first one as a pattern to cut the second one.
• From the fabric for the bows, cut four strips each 7½ x 32 inches.

Assembly

1. Fold each 7½ x 32-inch strip in half length-wise with right sides facing, and trim one end of each at a 45-degree angle as shown (Figure 1).

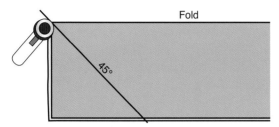

Figure 1
Fold bow strip and cut at 45-degree
angle from fold to cut edges.

2. Pin the short angled and long edges together and stitch ¼ inch from the pinned edges. Clip the point to eliminate bulk (Figure 2). Turn each tie right side out and press the finished edges carefully.

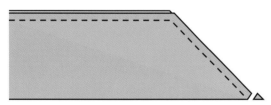

Figure 2
Stitch bow edges; trim point.

3. Position the short raw edges of each bow even with the pillow top long edges, spacing them as shown. Machine-baste in place (Figure 3).

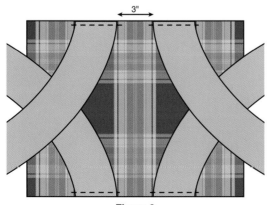

Figure 3
Baste bow strips to pillow top.

4. Position the fringe header in the seam allowance all the way around the pillow-top outer edge and pin. Machine-baste in place (Figure 4).

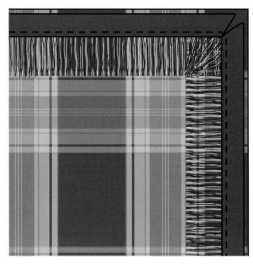

Figure 4
Sew fringe header
to seam allowance.

5. With right sides facing and the bow strips tucked completely inside and out of the way of the seam lines, machine-stitch ½ inch from the raw edges all around the pillow. Leave a 10-inch-long opening in one short end for turning.

6. Turn the pillow cover right side out. Turn in and press the opening edge on the back of the pillow cover.

7. Tuck the pillow form inside. It should be a firm, snug fit because the pillow-cover pieces were cut so they would actually be smaller than the pillow form after the two layers were stitched together. Slipstitch the turned-and-pressed edge of the opening to the fringe to finish.

8. Tie the strips into two bows. Hand-tack the bow layers together so they maintain their shape and don't come undone. ◆

Garden Delights

Floral appliques, pretty garden prints and hand-painted blossoms are right at home on designer pillows for your sunroom, porch or patio. They will help bring the sunshine in, even on a wintry day.

In the Garden

DESIGNS BY LORINE MASON

Coordinating checked, lattice and floral prints team up in these pretty pillows. Bias piping accents the edges of the woven strips and garden paths. In their crisp, clean colors, the pillows make perfect accents in a sunroom or cheery breakfast nook.

Finished Sizes
Garden Weave: 18 inches square
Along the Garden Path: 12 x 16 inches

Garden Weave

Materials for Garden Weave
- 54-inch-wide decorator fabrics
    1½ yards green-and-white check
    ⅝ yard coordinating floral botanical print
        on white background
- ⅝ yard cotton lining
- 14 yards ⁵⁄₃₂-inch-diameter white cotton cord
    for the strip piping
- 2½ yards ¹²⁄₃₂-inch-diameter white cotton
    cord for outer-edge welting
- 18-inch-square pillow form
- Rotary cutter, mat and ruler
- All-purpose thread to match fabrics
- Air- or water-soluble fabric marker
- Basic sewing tools and equipment

Cutting for Garden Weave
- From the green-and-white check, cut three
    19-inch squares, one for the pillow front

lining and two for the pillow back with
    envelope closure.
- From the remaining check fabric, cut enough
    1½-inch-wide bias strips to make 14 yards of
    bias piping for the ⁵⁄₃₂-inch-diameter cotton
    cord and enough 2-inch bias strips to make
    2½ yards of bias welting using the ¹²⁄₃₂-inch-
    diameter cotton cord. Use bias seams as
    shown on page 11 to join the strips into
    continuous lengths.
- From the floral botanical print, cut (12) 3½ x
    19-inch strips.
- From the cotton lining, cut (12) 3½ x
    19-inch strips.

Assembly for Garden Weave

Project Notes: *Use ½-inch-wide seam allowances unless otherwise directed.*

1. Refer to Making Fabric-Covered Welting on page 12. Create 2½ yards of bias welting for the outer edge of the pillow using the 2-inch-wide fabric strips and the 12/32-inch-diameter cotton cord. Create 14 yards of bias piping using the 1½-inch-wide fabric strips and the 5/32-inch-diameter cotton cord.

2. Cut the 14 yards of piping into 20-inch lengths.

3. Set four 3½ x 19-inch print strips aside for step 5. With raw edges even, sew a length of piping to the long edges of each of the remaining eight print strips. Use a contrast-color thread in the bobbin and adjust the zipper foot to the right of the needle so you can sew as close to the cord as possible (Figure 1).

Figure 1
Sew piping to long edges
of each floral strip.

4. With right sides facing and raw edges even, pin a 3½ x 19-inch cotton lining strip to each of the piped print strips. Pin in place along both edges. Turn over and stitch just inside the row of contrast basting on each long edge. It may feel as though you are crowding the cord, but you should be able to stitch a bit closer to the cord, just inside the basting. It's not necessary to remove the basting. Turn each lined strip right side out and press (Figure 2). Trim piping ends even with the fabric strips.

Figure 2
Make 8 strips with
piping on both long edges.

5. Repeat steps 3 and 4 with the four remaining strips, but sew piping to only one edge of each of the strips. Sew the lining to the piped edge of each strip as described above, and then turn the lining to the back of the strip and press. Machine-baste the long raw edges together a scant ⅜ inch from the raw edges.

6. Working on a large flat surface, use the fabric marker to draw center lines on the right side of one of the 18-inch squares. Position piped strips along each side of the vertical lines and weave the third and fourth strips over and under them with their edges meeting at the horizontal line. Pin the strips in place, making sure to keep them straight and perpendicular to the placement lines (Figure 3).

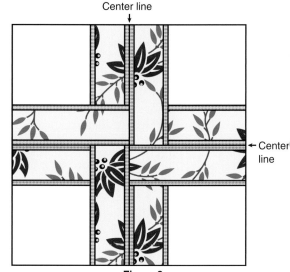

Figure 3
Begin weaving strips.

7. Continue weaving strips horizontally and vertically until you have covered the square with all but the last four strips. Pin the strips in place as you work. The outermost strip of each row will not have piping. Check the weaving to make sure all strips are straight and perpendicular to each other. Adjust as needed and then machine-baste a scant ½ inch from the raw edges to secure the woven strips to the checked square underneath (Figure 4).

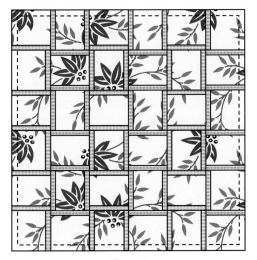

Figure 4
Completed Pillow Top

8. Turn under and press 1 inch along one edge of each of the remaining checked squares. Turn under and press an additional 3 inches. Edgestitch in place. Place the rectangles face up with the folded edges aligned, and then adjust one over the other so the resulting layered piece measures 19 inches square. Pin and baste the overlapped layers together (Figure 5).

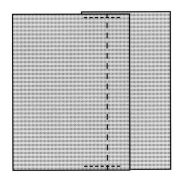

Figure 5
Overlap back panels
and baste together.

9. With right sides together and raw edges even, round the corners. Use a small saucer to mark the cutting line. Cut each corner on the marked line (Figure 6).

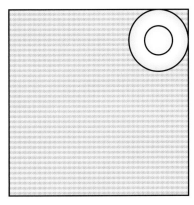

Figure 6
Trace around small saucer
to round corners.

10. Place contrasting thread in the bobbin and attach the zipper foot to the machine. Beginning with the turned end of the welting a few inches from one corner, pin and sew it to the right side of the woven pillow top. Start the sewing about 2 inches from one corner and make a neat join when you reach the point where you started (see page 12).

11. With right sides facing, sew the pillow back to the pillow front. Stitch with pillow top on top so you can see the basting and stitch just inside it as you did when constructing the piped strips for weaving. Serge- or zigzag-finish the seam allowance edges together.

12. Turn the pillow cover right side out and press as needed. Insert the pillow form.

Along the Garden Path

Materials for Along the Garden Path
• 54-inch-wide decorator fabrics
    ½ yard green-and-white check for pillow
      back, piping and welting
    ⅛ yard coordinating floral botanical print
      for garden paths
    ½ yard green-and-white coordinating
      geometric print for pillow front
• 1½ yards ⁵⁄₃₂-inch-diameter white cotton
    cord for piping
• 1¾ yards ¹²⁄₃₂-inch-diameter white cotton
    cord for welting
• 12 x 16-inch pillow form
• Air-soluble marking pen
• Rotary cutter, mat and ruler
• All-purpose thread to match fabrics
• Zipper foot
• Basic sewing tools and equipment

Cutting for Along the Garden Path
• From green-and-white check, cut two 10½ x
    13-inch rectangles. From the remaining
    fabric, cut enough 2-inch-wide bias strips
    to make a 1¾-yard-long piece for the outer-
    edge welting and enough 1½-inch bias strips
    to make a 1½-yard-long strip for the piping.
    Using bias seams as shown on page 11, sew

the strips of each width together to make
two long strips. Press the seams open.
• From the floral print, cut two 3½ x 13-inch strips.
• From the green-and-white geometric print, cut
    two 2½ x 13-inch strips and one 9 x 13-inch
    rectangle. If the print is not bias oriented, cut
    these pieces on the true bias (see Bias Finder
    below) and staystitch ⅜ inch from the raw
    edges of each piece to stabilize.

Assembly for Along the Garden Path
Project Notes: *Use ½-inch-wide seam allowances
unless otherwise directed.*

1. Refer to Making Fabric-Covered Welting on
page 12 to make 1½ yards of bias piping using
the 1½-inch-wide fabric strips and the ⁵⁄₃₂-inch-
diameter cord. Create 1¾ yards of bias welting
using the 2-inch-wide fabric strips and ¹²⁄₃₂-inch-
diameter cord.

2. With raw edges aligned, sew piping to each
long raw edge of each 3½ x 13-inch strip. Use
a contrasting color thread in the bobbin and a
zipper foot adjusted to the right of the needle to
stitch as close as possible to the cord.

3. With right sides facing, sew the piped strips to
the center panel for the pillow top. Stitch from
the wrong side of the piped strips so you can
stitch just inside the first stitching. Press the seam
allowances toward the piped strips (Figure 1).

Figure 1
Sew piped panels to center panel.

4. Add the 2½ x 13-inch green geometric strips to the pillow top in the same manner, and press the seam allowances toward the floral strips to complete the pillow top.

5. On each 10½ x 13-inch green-and-white check rectangle, turn under and press 2 inches at one short end. Turn again and press. Edgestitch the inner folded edge in place.

6. With the two pieces side by side and the folded edges meeting at the center, slip the left rectangle over the right and adjust so that the resulting layered rectangle for the pillow back measures 13 x 17 inches. Pin the layers together in the overlapped area to secure, and machine-baste the layers together ⅜ inch from the raw edges. Remove the pins (Figure 2).

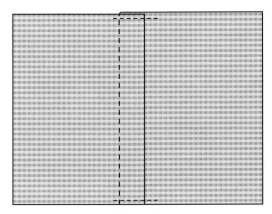

Figure 2
Overlay back
panels and baste layers together.

7. With right sides facing, arrange the layered pillow back on top of the pillow top and round the corners as shown for the Garden Weave pillow in Figure 6 on page 155.

8. Thread the bobbin with a contrasting-color thread and attach the zipper foot (or a piping foot if one is available for the cord size in the welting).

9. Beginning a few inches from one corner, pin welting to the right side of a long edge of the pillow top. Sew in place, making a neat join when you reach the beginning (see page 13).

10. Pin the pillow front with welting to the pillow back with right sides together. With the wrong side of the pillow top facing you, stitch just inside the first row of stitching, crowding the welting to stitch as close to the cord as possible.

11. Zigzag- or serge-finish the seam allowance raw edges together. Turn the pillow cover right side out and press. Insert the pillow form. ◆

Bias Finder

Cutting fabric on the bias is a design choice based on the fabric design and is not necessary if the fabric design is already printed on the bias.

1. To locate the true bias, fold the fabric so the selvage is aligned with one long straight edge and press lightly to mark the bias. Unfold and draw a line along the bias fold with the marking pen.

2. Measure and cut pillow sections using this line as you would the straight grain line.

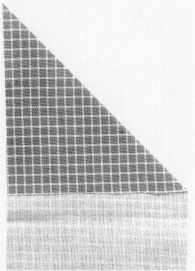

Flowers All Around

DESIGN BY CAROL ZENTGRAF

Trimmed with flowers, this cushy, box-edge silk pillow adds a romantic touch to your decor. The pleated panels are easy to create with shirring tape.

Finished Size
11 x 17 x 3 inches

Materials
- 44/45-inch-wide fabric
    1 yard brocade
    ⅓ yard contrasting or coordinating solid-
        color silk dupioni or similar synthetic fabric
- 1 yard cotton muslin for the pillow insert
- 4 yards lightweight 1¼-inch-wide shirring tape
- 2 yards flower trim
- All-purpose thread to match fabrics and trim
- Polyester fiberfill for the pillow form
- Permanent fabric adhesive
- Rotary cutter, mat and ruler
- Basic sewing tools and equipment

Cutting
- From the brocade, cut one 12 x 18-inch panel for the back, three 4 x 12-inch panels for the front, two 4 x 12-inch boxing strips and two 4 x 18-inch boxing strips.
- From the solid-color fabric, cut two 5½ x 30-inch panels for the front.
- From the muslin, cut two 12 x 18-inch panels for the pillow form front and back, two 4 x 12-inch boxing strips and two 4 x 18-inch boxing strips.

Note: *In lieu of shirring tape, substitute gathering by machine. See Gathers Instead on page 161.*

Assembly

Project Note: *Use ½-inch-wide seam allowances.*

1. To make the pillow form, sew the short muslin boxing strips between the long strips to make a circle. Sew the boxing strip to one muslin panel (see page 8), aligning the seams of the strips with the panel corners. Repeat to sew the remaining panel to the boxing strip, leaving an opening for turning and stuffing. Trim the corners, turn right side out and press.

2. Stuff the form with polyester fiberfill to the desired firmness, and sew the opening closed by hand or machine-stitch the opening closed as shown on page 8 (Figure 1).

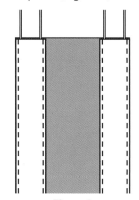

Figure 1
Make muslin pillow insert.

3. To shirr each solid-color panel for the pillow top, sew shirring tape along both long edges of the panel wrong side, stitching along each outer edge of the tape. Be sure to place the drawstring pockets on the tape at the same position on each side of the panel (Figure 2).

Figure 2
Stitch shirring tape to each long edge of solid-color panels.

4. Knot the drawstring cords together at one end of each piece of shirring tape. At the other end, pull the cords to pleat the fabric strip down to a 12-inch-long piece. Knot the cords securely and trim away the excess cord at each end. Adjust the fullness evenly in each panel and press. Machine-baste ⅜ inch from each long edge of each panel to secure the pleats.

5. Arrange the shirred panels with the brocade panels for the pillow front and sew together. Press the seams toward the brocade strips (Figure 3).

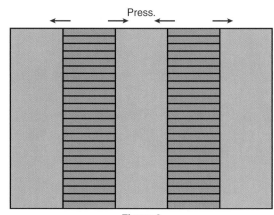

Figure 3
Sew pillow front panels together.

6. Prepare the boxing strip and attach it to the pillow front as directed for the pillow form in step 1 above. Sew the pillow back to the remaining raw edge of the boxing strip, leaving an 8-inch-long opening in one long edge for turning. Trim the corners and turn the pillow cover right side out.

7. Insert the pillow form and slipstitch the opening edges together.

8. Beginning in the center of one long edge of the pillow, apply a line of fabric adhesive along the center of the boxing strip and press the center of the flower trim into the adhesive. Continue around the pillow, working in 6–8-inch-long sections at a time. Cut and glue a strip of flower trim along the center front of the pillow. Tuck the cut ends under the trim on the boxing strip and glue in place. ◆

Gathers Instead

If you prefer a softer, less structured look, eliminate the shirring tape and gather the shirring strips instead.

1. Machine baste ¼ inch and ½ inch from the long edges of each shirring strip. When you begin each row of basting, backstitch for two or three stitches to anchor the basting.

2. Draw up the basting on each edge of each shirring strip so the resulting strip is 12 inches long.

3. Tie off the threads securely.

4. Adjust the gathers in each strip so they are straight and perpendicular to the long edges. It also helps to tug the gathers across the strip.

5. When satisfied with appearance of the shirred strips, machine baste again ½ inch from the raw edges.

6. Sew the strips to the pillow pieces as directed for the pleated strips as directed for the pleated strips.

Garden-Fresh Iris

DESIGN BY DIANE BUNKER

Create the look of needlepoint without all the hand stitching. The secret is stenciling your favorite flowers over a piece of needlepoint canvas. Austrian crystals add the sparkle of fresh raindrops to this decorative pillow.

Finished Size
14 x 28 inches

Materials
- ½ yard 45-inch-wide off-white linen or linen like fabric for the iris panel
- ½ yard 54-inch-wide decorator fabric for the borders and pillow back
- ½ yard needlepoint canvas, 12 stitches to the inch
- ⅞ yard 3-inch-wide decorative fringe trim
- ⅞ yard ⅜- or ½-inch-wide contrast soutache trim
- 14-inch-long invisible zipper
- All-purpose thread to match fabrics
- 14 x 28-inch knife-edge pillow form
- Clear monofilament thread
- Pencil
- Plaid Stencil Decor #26872 Iris or other stencil of your choice
- 8½ x 11-inch sheet clear acetate
- Textile medium
- Deco Art paints
    - Lavender
    - Dioxazine Purple
    - Cadmium Yellow
    - Burnt Sienna
    - Evergreen
    - Hauser Medium Green
    - Paper Effects Pearl Gold
- #10 flat brush
- 2 (¼-inch) stencil brushes
- 2 (½-inch) stencil brushes
- Painter's tape
- Paper towels
- Basic fabric painting and stenciling tools and supplies
- Black permanent-ink marking pen
- Bejeweler iron-on rhinestone setter
- 10 (4mm) gold Swarovski crystal rhinestones
- 60 (6mm) topaz Swarovski crystal rhinestones
- Zipper foot
- Rotary cutter, mat and ruler
- Basic sewing tools and equipment

Cutting

- From the off-white linen, cut one 15 x 19-inch rectangle for the pillow front.
- From the decorator fabric, cut two 6 x 15-inch side panels and one 15 x 29-inch back panel.
- From the needlepoint canvas, cut one 17 x 19-inch rectangle.

Stenciling Tips

Read through these tips before you begin the stenciling process for the pillow front. If you have never done any stenciling, it is essential to practice the techniques with scrap fabric and needlepoint canvas before you stencil the pillow panel.

• Be sure you have at least one brush for each color family, or in this case, one brush for the purples for the irises, one for the gold for the iris beards, and one for green for the leaves.

• Add a puddle of textile medium next to your paint colors. Dip your brush into the medium and then into the paint.

• On a DRY paper towel and in a circular motion, remove a lot of the paint. This is called blotting in the stenciling directions.

• Before you add paint to any stencil, make sure there is enough of a bridge between different colors to be stenciled. (A bridge is the space between the different parts.)

• When you begin stenciling, always start at the outer edges of the design and work your way toward the center. This keeps the centers lighter for a more natural look.

• Use a pouncing motion rather than a brushing motion so the paint works through the holes in the needlepoint canvas.

• No matter what the technique, you should always start with a light touch and check under the stencil and canvas to see how it looks so you can adjust your pouncing pressure to get the desired results.

Stenciling the Irises

Note: *This design calls for a little manipulating of the stencil, meaning the outer flowers and leaves are done by turning the clean, dry stencil over and angling it outward to position the outer flowers and leaves on each side. You will also use only two special leaves to get the end leaves and one of the longer leaves. When repositioning you will need to take special care in taping on top of existing leaves and petals before adding the paint to the new ones.*

1. Read Stenciling Tips before you begin and test your technique on scraps first. Refer to the iris pillow photo close-up for help with color placement as you work your way through the following steps.

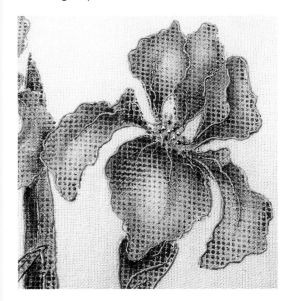

2. Fold the linen panel in half crosswise and mark the fold at each cut edge to mark the center.

3. Using painter's tape, tape the panel to a hard, flat surface. Tape all four edges with the tape straight and ½ inch from the edges to make it easy to reposition the panel when you lift it to check your work. Keep the fabric straight and on grain (Figure 1).

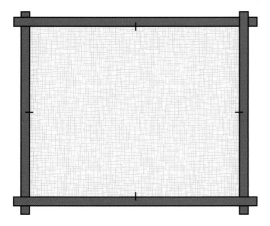

Figure 1
Tape Linen to work surface.

4. Position the needlepoint canvas on top with the upper edge just above the upper edge of the fabric. Add a piece of tape at the bottom of the needlepoint canvas even with the tape on the fabric. This will also help in your repositioning. Use several short pieces of tape at each short end of the linen panel to secure the canvas edges.

5. Refer to the Placement Guide on page 168 and to the photo. Begin with stencil A. Tape the stencil to the canvas so that the tallest iris is about 1 inch from the upper edge of the fabric and the center of the stencil is about ½ inch to the left of the center of the panel. Don't worry that this section of the stencil is too long for the fabric panel.

6. Pounce the beards of the two center irises using Cadmium Yellow and textile medium. Be sure to blot the tool before pouncing. Pounce the leaves next with Hauser Medium Green and textile medium. Blot first and then apply, pouncing around the edges first. Next, without cleaning the brush, move to the Evergreen color and add textile medium. Pounce the areas where the leaves need to be the darkest—where petals and leaves overlap each other.

7. Cover the beards with small pieces of tape to protect them while you stencil the flowers. Use

Lavender plus textile medium to pounce the two iris flowers. Pounce harder at the outer edge so they are darker than the interior sections. With the same brush, pick up some Dioxazine Purple plus textile medium and blot before pouncing the iris again, this time paying careful attention to the areas that should be darker, such as where petals overlap and where they begin in the centers. Remove the A stencil.

8. Position the B stencil, using the dashed lines to assist you. Secure with tape. Pounce as you did when using stencil A. Pay close attention to how close the right leaf is to the iris and cover the area with tape so you don't get green paint on the iris. Add tape to the leaf so you won't get purple paint where you don't want it on the leaf.

9. Remove the stencil when you have finished pouncing. Position stencil C and add tape to prevent getting paint where it is not wanted. By now you should have completed the two center irises.

10. Clean the stencils using a soft sponge to remove the paint. Wipe them off to remove water.

11. Add irises to the left and right of the center irises in the same manner, always beginning with stencil A and ending with stencil C. For the iris to the left, use the shorter iris in reverse and angle it slightly to the left (see the pillow photo). Take your time and think about the design. It may help to tape over the flowers and leaves you are not using to avoid confusion. The leaf next to the left-hand iris is on the reverse side of stencil B. The leaf farthest to the left is on the front of stencil A. Use only the upper portion of the center leaf. When flipping stencils, be sure to clean the paint first so you don't damage the previously stenciled designs. For the iris to the right of center, use the taller iris in reverse and the leaf next to it—find them on stencil A. For the long leaf between, use the longest leaf on stencil C. To use this leaf, begin at the bottom of the leaf and line it up so the small plastic bridge on the stencil covers up the one finished leaf on the fabric. Pounce the color in place and then carefully move the stencil up until you see the tip of the leaf just above the iris. Pounce color in the tip. When you remove the stencil, you will see that a piece of the leaf is missing. Simply tape to the outer edges right on top of the canvas to define that area and pounce again. For the last leaf, use the leaf on the right side of stencil A. When you have completed the stenciling, remove the needlepoint canvas and clean the stencils.

12. Add more color and depth to the stenciled design (without the stencil in place) by lightly daubing colors in a circular motion.

13. To give the leaves a realistic look, add veins. First, place the piece of plastic on top of the stencil and outline each leaf with the marking pen. Add a vein through the center of each one and label A, B or C. Mark the top of each leaf with an X (Figure 2). Cut on the lines to create the stencils for the veins (Figure 3).

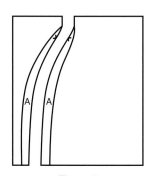

Figure 3
Cut on lines to create
stencils for veins.

14. Decide which side (left or right) of each leaf you want to be the darkest. Use the correct side of plastic needed to achieve the shading for that leaf. On the next reversed leaf you might want the other side to be darker. Place the appropriate leaf stencil in place over each stenciled leaf and pounce on color to darken one side of each leaf.

15. To make the completed design really pop, wet a #10 flat brush, blot it and dip into the textile medium. Next, dip one corner of the brush into one of the darker colors. Use Dioxazine Purple for shading the irises and Burnt Sienna for shading the beards. Use Evergreen to shade the leaves and stems. Before you take the paint-filled brush to the fabric, blend it by brushing the bristles back and forth a few times on your palette paper to mix the paint and medium together. Use the paint-filled brush to add shadows to the petals, beards, leaves and stems where they overlap each other and to any other areas you think should be a little darker. Lightly tint a few of the leaf tips with a little purple, but make sure there is hardly any color on your brush when you do this.

16. Outline the completed design with Paper Effects Pearl Gold and the special needle tip provided. Refer to the photo for accent line placement. Note that this tip clogs easily, so

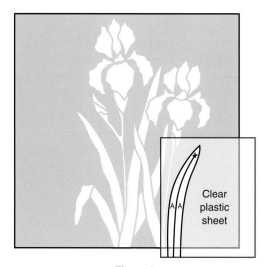

Figure 2
Trace leaves and add veins.

keep the tiny pin that comes in it handy. Practice outlining on a piece of scrap fabric before outlining the design on the stenciled panel.

Pillow Assembly

***Note:** Use ½-inch-wide seam allowances.*

1. Refer to Figure 4 for steps 1–4. With right sides facing, sew the side panels to the short ends of the stenciled panel. Press the seam allowances toward the side panels.

2. Pin the soutache trim in place with one edge along each seam line and sew in place using the clear monofilament thread and a long, wide zigzag stitch.

3. Before cutting the fringe into two pieces, find the center and wrap with a piece of painter's tape to prevent raveling. Cut through the center and leave the tape in place.

4. With right sides facing and the fringe ends toward the pillow center, sew the fringe header to the short ends of the pillow front. Remove the tape at the fringe ends.

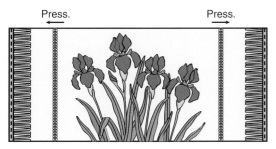

Figure 4
Sew side panels to center. Add soutache
trim at seam lines; add fringe at ends.

5. Insert the invisible zipper between one short end of the pillow front and back panels. See Invisible Zipper Installation on page 16.

6. ***Unzip the zipper*** and pin the pillow front to the back along the raw edges, making sure the fringe ends are not caught in the seam allowances. Stitch ½ inch from the raw edges. Clip across the corners. Serge- or zigzag-finish the seam-allowance raw edges together. Turn the pillow cover right side out through the zipper opening.

7. Embellish the iris centers and the side panels with rhinestones as desired. Use the 4mm gold rhinestones on the beard of each iris. Use 6mm topaz rhinestones on the side panels for raindrops. Follow the manufacturer's directions to apply them.

8. Insert the pillow form and zip the zipper. ◆

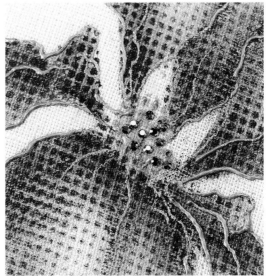

**Faux Needlepoint Iris Pillow
Placement Guide**

X's indicate the natural front of the stencil; this is where you begin
– – – Dash marks indicate tape is needed.
Zigzags indicate where to shade.
Lines down center of leaves are veins you wil cut out of the clear plastic.

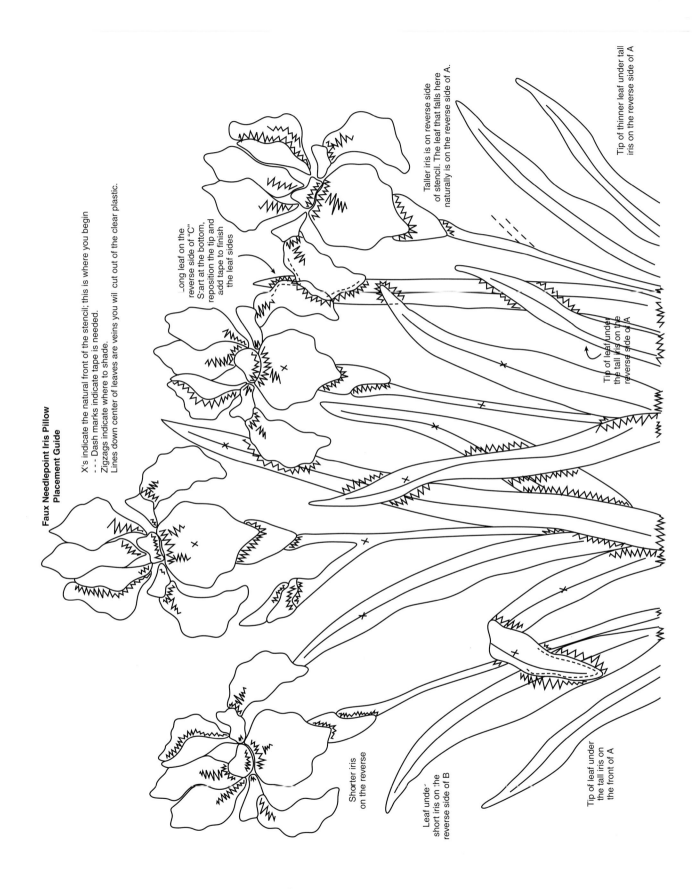

...ong leaf on the
reverse side of "C"
S:art at the bottom,
reposition the tip and
add tape to finish
the leaf sides

Taller iris is on reverse side
of stencil. The leaf that falls here
naturally is on the reverse side of A.

Tip of thinner leaf under tall
iris on the reverse side of A

Tip of leaf under
the tall iris on the
reverse side of A

Shorter iris
on the reverse

Leaf unde-
short iris on the
reverse side of B

Tip of leaf under
the tall iris on
the front of A

Floral Fantasy

DESIGN BY CAROL ZENTGRAF

A swirling vine with faux suede blossoms flows across the silk cover on this pretty pillow. Beautiful ready-made trim—or handmade silk flowers if you prefer—accents the edge.

Finished Size
18 inches square

Materials
- ⅝ yard cream silk dupioni
- 8 (4-inch) squares assorted colors faux suede for flowers
- 5 (2 x 4-inch) rectangles green faux suede for leaves
- 2 (19-inch) squares knit or weft-insertion fusible interfacing
- 2¼ yards decorative flower-and-ribbon trim
- 2½ yards ¼-inch-diameter twisted decorative cord
- 18-inch-square knife-edge pillow form
- Self-adhesive, double-sided basting tape
- Permanent fabric adhesive
- Air-soluble fabric marker
- Tracing paper
- Cording foot for sewing machine if available; substitute an open-toe embroidery foot
- Optional: Invisible zipper and invisible zipper foot
- Rotary cutter, mat and ruler
- Basic sewing tools and equipment

Cutting
- From the cream silk, cut two 19-inch squares. Follow the manufacturer's directions to apply the interfacing squares to the wrong side of the silk squares.
- Trace the flower and leaf patterns onto tracing paper and cut out. Cut eight assorted flowers in the faux suede colors of your choice and five leaves from the green faux suede.

Assembly

1. Refer to Figure 1 and use the air-soluble fabric marker to draw a flowing vine on the right side of one of the interfaced silk squares. Keep the line at least 2 inches from the fabric edge. Cut a length of cord the same length as the vine.

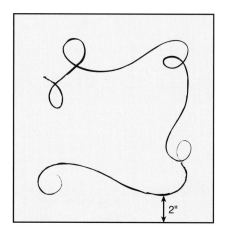

Figure 1
Draw vine on silk square no
closer than 2 inches to the edges.

2. Adjust the sewing machine for a zigzag stitch slightly wider than the twisted cord. Attach the cording foot. Beginning at one end of the drawn vine, insert the cord end under the foot and zigzag over it as you guide the cord along the line. The zigzag stitches should trap the cord underneath as shown in Figure 2. If you don't have a cording foot, guide the cord between the toes of an open-toe embroidery foot. Make sure the cord is smooth and the silk is not puckered—tugging gently along the cord will help eliminate puckers. Stitch back and forth several times at each end to cover the raw cord.

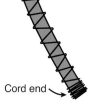

Cord end

Figure 2
Zigzag over cord to
couch in place.

3. Referring to the pillow photo, layer the suede flower shapes to make five different blossoms. Use permanent fabric adhesive to glue the centers of the layered flowers together. Position the flowers along the vine and tack in place with a dot of fabric adhesive. Add veins to each petal in contrasting thread by stitching two lines on each petal. End the stitching ½–¾ inch from the outer petal edge (Figure 3).

Figure 3
Add stitched veins
to flower petals.

4. Position and tack the leaves along the vine in the same manner as the flowers. Cut a 2½–3½-inch length of cord for each leaf vein/stem and couch in place. Allow the leaf to gather a bit as you stitch to create a dimensional effect. End each leaf vein/stem alongside the vine and stitch back and forth over the raw ends as you did for the vine (Figure 4).

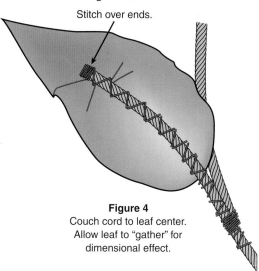

Stitch over ends.

Figure 4
Couch cord to leaf center.
Allow leaf to "gather" for
dimensional effect.

5. Optional: For a removable pillow cover, insert an invisible zipper (see page 16) in one seam. ***Unzip the zipper*** before completing the remainder of the seam all around the pillow cover. Otherwise, sew the pillow front to the back all around, leaving an 8-inch opening for turning. Turn the cover right side out and turn under and press the opening edges. Insert the pillow form and slipstitch the opening closed.

6. Use fabric adhesive to glue the flower-and-ribbon trim around the outer edge of the pillow.

Note: *If you prefer, make silk flowers and leaves for the pillow perimeter and sew or glue in place. Consult a ribbon-flower book for how-tos.*

7. Embellish the flower centers on the pillow top with small pieces cut from the leftover trim. Glue pieces to the center of the flower. ◆

Floral Fantasy Templates
Actual Size

Fabric & Supplies

Page 24: *Gold Rush*—The Warm Co. Warm & Natural batting, Fairfield Processing Corp. Soft Touch pillow forms, Adhesive Products Inc. The Ultimate! Glue

Page 32: *Scrollwork*—Fairfield Processing Corp. Soft Touch pillow form

Page 35: *Tailored in Suede*—Fairfield Processing Corp. Soft Touch pillow form

Page 38: *Framed Jewels*—Fairfield Processing Corp. Poly-Fil polyester fiberfill and Soft Touch pillow forms

Page 43: *Color Caravan*—Fairfield Processing Corp. Pop-in Pillow Insert, Adhesive Products Inc. The Ultimate! Glue, The Warm Co. Warm & Natural needled cotton batting, Sulky of America 30-weight rayon embroidery thread

Page 57: *Diamond Sophisticate*—Fairfield Processing Corp. feather pillow form

Page 61: *Road to Marrakech*—Fairfield Processing Corp. Soft Touch Pillow form

Page 68: *Hurrah for the Red, White & Blue*—Fairfield Processing Corp. Soft Touch pillow forms

Page 74: *Per-Sueded*—Toile Center and Toile Corner embroidery designs. Fairfield Processing Corp. Soft Touch pillow form

Page 90: *Ships Ahoy*—Fairfield Processing Corp. NU-Foam upholstery foam alternative

Page 100: *Tutti Frutti* — Fairfield Processing Corp. Soft Touch pillow form

Page 117: *Boudoir Beauties*—Beacon Adhesives Fabri-Tac permanent fabric adhesive, Prym Dritz Wonder Tape, Fairfield Processing Corp. Soft Touch pillow forms, Jackman's Fabrics fabric and trim, Exotic Silks/Thai Silks silk dupioni fabric

Page 122: *Floral Romance*—Fairfield Processing Corp. Soft Touch pillow form

Page 132: *Provence Country Chic*—Beacon Adhesive Fabri-Tac permanent fabric adhesive, Expo International, Inc. tassel and gimp trims, Fairfield Processing Corp. Soft Touch pillow form, French Connections French Provençal fabric

Pages 148: *Bow Regards*—Fairfield Processing Corp. Soft Touch pillow form

Page 152: *In the Garden*—Fairfield Processing Corp. Soft Touch pillow forms

Page 158: *Flowers All Around*—Beacon Adhesives Fabri-Tac permanent fabric adhesive, Exotic Silks/Thai Silks silk brocade and silk dupioni fabric, Expo International Inc. flower trim, Fairfield Processing Corp. Poly-Fil polyester fiberfill

Page 163: *Garden-Fresh Iris*—Plaid Stencil Décor #26872 Iris, Deco Art paints

Page 169: *Floral Fantasy*—Beacon Adhesives Fabri-Tac permanent fabric adhesive, Prym-Dritz Wonder Tape, Expo International flower and ribbon trim, Fairfield Processing Corp. Soft Touch pillow form, Exotic Silks/Thai Silks silk dupioni fabric, Toray Ultrasuede (America) Inc. Ultrasuede fabric

Sewing Services

The following companies provided fabric and/or supplies for projects in this book. If you are unable to locate a product locally, contact the manufacturers listed below for the closest retail or mail-order source in your area.

Adhesive Products Inc.
www.crafterspick.com

Beacon Adhesives
(914) 699-3400
www.beaconcreates.com

Conso Products
(800) 845-2431
www.conso.com

Deco Art
(800) 367-3047
www.decoart.com

Embroidery Library
www.emblibrary.com

Exotic/Thai Silks
(800) 722-7455
www.thaisilks.com

Expo International
(800) 542-4367
www.expointl.com

Fairfield Processing Corp.
(800) 980-8000
www.poly-fil.com

French Connections
(919) 545-9296
www.french-nc.com

Jackman's Fabrics
(800) 758-3742
www.jackmanfabrics.com

Moda Fabrics
www.modafabrics.com

Plaid Enterprises
www.plaidonline.com

Prym-Dritz Corp.
www.dritz.com

Sulky of America
(800) 874-4115
www.sulky.com

The Warm Co.
(800) 234-9276
www.warmcompany.com

Waverly Fabrics
www.waverly.com

Toray Ultrasuede
(732) 431-1550
www.ultrasuede.com

Special Thanks

We would like to thank the talented sewing designers whose work is featured in this collection.

Marta Alto
Bow Regards, 148
Per-Sueded, 74

Pam Archer
Gold Rush, 24

Janice Bullis
Road to Marrakech, 61
Vintage Pleats, 85

Diane Bunker
Garden-Fresh Iris, 163

Karen Dillon
Hurrah for the Red,
    White & Blue, 68

Stephanie Corina Goddard
Ships Ahoy, 90

Linda Turner Griepentrog
Color Caravan, 43

Pam Lindquist
Elegant in Ecru, 108
Diamond Sophisticate, 57
Gypsy's Dream, 80
Man-Tailored & Elegant, 32

Lorine Mason
In the Garden, 152

Carol Moffatt
Raggity Taggity, 143

Judy Murrah
Elegantly Patched, 128

Lynn Weglarz
Beautifully Enveloped, 52

Barbara Weiland
Eight Is Enough, 96
Floral Romance, 122
Framed Jewels, 38
Mixed Media, 64
Tutti Frutti, 100

Carol Zentgraf
Boudoir Beauties, 117
Floral Fantasy, 169
Flowers All Around, 158
Provence Country Chic, 132